Mario J. A. Bartolini holds a master's degree in political history from the Université de Sherbrooke and a master's degree in war studies from the Royal Military College of Canada. He has published on Roman military history, specifically on the evolution of the great strategy of defense of the Roman Empire and on intelligence-related activities carried out under the imperial regime. Now retired, he served as an officer in the Canadian Forces Reserve, and his professional career of 24 years was in the field of public safety and national security.

Ad augusta per angusta…

Mario J.A. Bartolini

THE SPECULATORES:
THE MEN WHO SPIED
FOR ROME

AUSTIN MACAULEY PUBLISHERS™

LONDON • CAMBRIDGE • NEW YORK • SHARJAH

Ordering Information
Quantity sales: Special discounts are available on quantity purchases by corporations, associations, and others. For details, contact the publisher at the address below.

Publisher's Cataloging-in-Publication data
Bartolini, Mario J.A.
The Speculatores: The Men Who Spied for Rome

ISBN 9798889106920 (Paperback)
ISBN 9798889106937 (Hardback)
ISBN 9798889106944 (ePub e-book)

Library of Congress Control Number: 2023921635

www.austinmacauley.com/us

First Published 2024
Austin Macauley Publishers LLC
40 Wall Street, 33rd Floor, Suite 3302
New York, NY 10005
USA

mail-usa@austinmacauley.com
+1 (646) 5125767

From the same author

Petit dictionnaire chronologique illustré des empereurs romains (Guérin) 2000.

Les causes du changement de la grande stratégie de défense périphérique à la défense en profondeur au IVe siècle (Vol 17, The Ancient History Bulletin) 2003.

Ammien Marcellin et le renseignement extérieur romain 353-378 après J.-C. (Vol 24, Scripta Mediterranea) 2003.

Apport stratégique au déclin de l'armée romaine (No 12-13, Histoire antique) 2004.

Procope (325-366 après J.-C.) d'après Ammien Marcellin (No 31, Histoire antique) 2007.

Roman Emperors: A Guide to the Men who Ruled the Empire (Pen & Sword Books) 2023.

The Men who Ruled the World from Rome (ancient-origins.net) 2023.

Procopius, Fourth Century AD Spy who Became a Roman Emperor (ancient-origins.net) 2023.

The Military Anarchy Period of the Roman Empire: Decent into Hades 235-250 AD (ancient-origins.net) 2023.

A Crumbling Roman Empire: Treachery, Mutiny and Plague 250-270 AD (ancient-origins.net) 2023.

Third-Century Roman Empire: Revival from Chaos 270-285 AD (ancient-origins.net) 2023.

Diocletian's Utopia: The Tetrarchy of the Roman Empire 285-325 AD (ancient-origins.net) 2023.

The Fall of the Western Roman Empire: A Military Perspective 405-455 AD (ancient-origins.net) 2023.

Desperate Lesser-Known Emperors Facing A Disintegrating Western Roman Empire 455-476 AD (ancient-origins.net) 2023.

Table of Contents

Abstract

For the past few decades, scholars of Ancient Roman history have displayed a modest but promising interest in the study of intelligence-related activities to determine their role on the internal management of the Roman State and in the development of its grand strategy of defense. Most of these academics agree that Roman leaders during the period of the Republic (509–27 BCE) did not seem to be motivated in investing in the development of state-sponsored intelligence activities, but that they did begin to show interest during the period following the inauguration of the imperial regime in 27 BCE. There is also a general consensus that supports the concept that the emperors of the Dominate Period (284–476 CE) had become consistent consumers of intelligence; the mid-fourth century corresponding to the 'Golden Age' of Roman intelligence-related activities.

Yet, there is currently no consensus in terms of acknowledging the existence of external or foreign intelligence activities (espionage) conducted by the Romans. In light of this curious conjuncture, this book aims to identify the causes behind this dissention and ultimately takes position on the rationality which questions the existence of Roman espionage activities.

To accomplish this undertaking, this book first examines the catalysts for the development of Roman intelligence activities and how these activities evolved from the Late Republic until the fourth century, a period during which indications of espionage activities, which we believe have been mostly misinterpreted by modern historians, become apparent. Subsequently, the second part of the book consists of an in-depth analysis, through an intelligence-focused lens, of the most reliable source of the fourth century on the topic: the surviving eighteen books of the *Res Gestae* written by Ammianus Marcellinus. As a Roman staff officer and historian of the second half of the fourth century, Ammianus was a reliable witness of the presumed 'Golden Age' of Roman espionage activities. The intent of this book is to demonstrate that by this time, the Romans were very much engaged in espionage.

Mario J. A. Bartolini holds a master's degree in political history from the Université de Sherbrooke and a master's degree in war studies from the Royal Military College of Canada. He has published on Roman military history, specifically on the evolution of the great strategy of defense of the Roman Empire and on intelligence-related activities carried out under the imperial regime. Now retired, he served as an officer in the Canadian Forces Reserve, and his professional career of 24 years was in the field of public safety and national security. His military experience as a reservist in an armor reconnaissance regiment and his employment as an intelligence officer have enabled him to provide knowledgeable insights into these types of activities that were conducted by the Ancient Romans.

Introduction

For the past several decades, scholars have shown an interest in the study of the grand strategy of the Roman Empire.[1] Some argue that, throughout classical Roman history, Roman leaders failed to establish a grand military strategy. For example, some historians argue that military decisions were made on an *ad hoc* basis by Roman authorities who reacted to political and military events rather than planning at the strategic level.[2] Some authors will even go as far as suggesting that Roman survival was reduced to pure luck.[3] At the other end of the spectrum of opinion, there is another group of historians who argue that the notion of a grand defense strategy existed among the Romans as early as the Republican Period.[4] Halfway between these two poles, there are other researchers who propose that 'in sum, if the Roman Republic lacked a coherent strategy in the sense of a great 'master plan' for Empire, this does not exclude strategy in general for how to defend it.'[5] Moreover, efforts have remained modest with regard to the study of intelligence and its role in the development of this grand strategy. It seems that this gap is also present in the study of Roman foreign relations in general. This seems surprising for a subject of such importance.[6]

Among the scholars who have exhibited an interest in the study of Roman intelligence activities, most agree that although Roman leaders during the period of the Republic (509–27 BCE) did not seem to be motivated in investing in the development of state sponsored intelligence activities; their successors did begin to show interest during the period following the inauguration of the imperial regime in 27 BCE. There is also a general consensus among these scholars proposing that the emperors of the Dominate Period (284–476 CE) had become consistent consumers of intelligence; the mid-fourth century corresponding to the 'Golden Age' of Roman intelligence-related activities. Yet, there is currently no consensus in terms of acknowledging the existence of external, or foreign, intelligence activities (espionage) conducted by the Romans. In light of this curious conjuncture, this book is aimed at identifying the motives behind this dissention and to ultimately take position on the rationality which questions the existence of Roman espionage activities.

To accomplish this undertaking, this book first examines the catalysts for the development of Roman intelligence activities and how these activities evolved from the Late Republic until the fourth century, a period during which indications of espionage activities, which we believe have been mostly misinterpreted by modern historians, become apparent. Subsequently, the second part of the book consists of an in-depth analysis, through an intelligence-focused lens, of the most reliable source of the fourth century on the topic: the surviving eighteen books of the *Res Gestae* written by Ammianus Marcellinus.

As a Roman staff officer and historian of the second half of the fourth century, Ammianus was a reliable witness of the presumed 'Golden Age' of Roman espionage activities. The intent of this book is to demonstrate that by this time, the Romans were very much engaged in espionage.

The *Res Gestae* has long been recognized as the major formal history, comparable to those of better-known writers from earlier periods. However, it seems that the *Res Gestae* has not received as much attention from modern scholars as have the traditional classical works. Some historians explain that the main reason for this is the fact that modern scholars have been mainly focused on the history of the church or on attempting to understand the causes of the decline and fall of the Roman Empire.[7] Possibly because it hardly deals with either of those subjects specifically, the *Res Gestae* does not seem to have received as much scholarly attention as other better-known classical works.

We begin our analysis with some important contextual details and a brief chronological overview of the development of the Roman state's grand strategy of defense. Within this framework, we will then proceed to describe the main institutional mechanisms and factors present in the Empire that were the catalysts for the development of intelligence-related activities before examining the various organizations carrying out these activities that emerged from this environment. We will then elaborate on depicted examples of special operations and of what we believe were espionage activities carried out by the Romans in the second half of the fourth century. We will then pursue with a series of descriptions of who might be characterized as the main spymasters of this period before drawing our conclusions. We intend to demonstrate that intelligence was an integral part of the decision-making process of the Roman authorities internally, in foreign relations and in military affairs.[8] In our view, espionage is still an under-appreciated topic in the studies of the Roman Empire.

Before pursuing, in order to ensure a common reference base, basic definitions are in order. In terms of a general definition of intelligence, we propose the following two, which are complementary: The *Intelligence Essentials for Everyone* describes it as being 'the continual collection, verification, and analysis of information that allows us to understand the problem or situation in actionable terms and then tailor a product in the context of the customer's circumstances.' [9] On a more practical level, the *CIA Insider's Dictionary* defines intelligence as 'the product resulting from the collecting and processing of information concerning actual and potential situations and conditions relating to domestic and foreign activities.'[10]

In terms of defining what espionage is, we propose the definition found in the *CIA Insider's Dictionary* which explains it as being 'the product resulting from the collecting and processing of information concerning actual and potential situations and conditions relating to foreign activities and to foreign or enemy-held areas.'[11] In a more practical sense, espionage, as it is used in a military or political setting, is simply the planning, the collection, the analysis and dissemination of information as related to forces, nations or coalitions of powers other than one's own.[12] It is important to remember that intelligence-related activities, whether these are conducted internally or are espionage undertakings, can be conducted in peace time or in times of war.

It is also useful to be reminded that the nature and needs of intelligence in Roman times, in an era long before the technological innovations with which we are familiar, were different from those of our own time. Lacking modern means and tools, the art of intelligence among the Ancient Romans depended almost exclusively on the human factor. The movement of information in pre-industrial societies was dependent on the movement of people. The transmission of information was determined by human interaction in a region or between regions: Interaction denoted information movement.[13] It was not until the second half of the nineteenth century, with the advent of the railway, telegraphic communications and the hot air balloon, that the nature of intelligence began to change.[14] Moreover, the Roman reality and needs in the realm of intelligence were mainly military in nature. Modern intelligence concerns, such as economic, technological and scientific espionage as well as counterterrorism, did not exist at that time. This preliminary reminder may seem obvious, but it remains nevertheless useful to ensure the safeguarding of a realistic conception of the Roman context of espionage throughout our analysis, thus limiting the possibilities of more thrilling but anachronistic Ian Fleming-inspired interpretations.

Modern historians outline five challenges associated with the study of Roman intelligence-related activities.[15] The first is that sources generally had only one origin. There are very few intelligence incidents that were reported simultaneously by both the Romans and their opponents, the main ones being the Germanic peoples and the Parthians, later called Persians. [16] Frequently, Rome's enemies, such as the Germanic peoples, were illiterate and left no texts. In the case of the Parthians and then Persians, there are very few written sources from them that have survived the tribulations of history. It must be added that the Iranian tradition of this period was fundamentally oral. Persian literary sources presenting this perspective are simply not available. Interestingly, it is mainly with the help of Greek and Roman sources that we have been able to learn about the history of this part of the world in late antiquity. [17]

The second challenge is related to the absence of a political will among the Romans to hide or minimize the use of military force. In fact, there were no restrictions on the use of force, no international laws or media to justify a need to conceal anything. Consequently, for the Romans, who were militarily the strongest, there was no threatening incentive to develop or utilize alternative methods, such as espionage, to gain a superiority, whether strategic, operational or tactical, that they already possessed. [18] Generally, until the fourth century, Rome usually resorted to the use of force, or the projection of force. However, from that time onward, when Rome found herself more and more often in situations of military disadvantage, as we shall see later, she would resort to a range of other means, including espionage.

The third challenge is the absence of a centralized Roman intelligence archive. We have no historical reference to suggest that there was a central office where such documents could have been stored.

Portico of the Library of Celsus in Ephesus, Turkey

The fourth complication was the apparent willingness of the Romans to conceal the practice of clandestine operations or activities that went against tradition. In what is termed the 'Roman propaganda line,'[19] the Romans showed contempt for the use of subterfuge, seeing themselves as descendants of Latin peasants with a disdain for anything artificial or dishonest. In their view, espionage activities were in the realm of subterfuge, as were deception and concealment.[20] These values, deeply rooted in the collective psyche, and this societal conservatism acted to venerate military strength as opposed to cheating.[21]

Finally, the last factor limiting the existence of intelligence sources is the fact that, except for the Parthian and later Persian Empire, until the middle of the fourth century, Rome did not have a sufficiently formidable enemy to deal with for which the military option was too risky. This observation also applies to the exploitation of intelligence by the Romans against this type of enemy. Although it remained in second place behind the Persian peril, we believe it is useful to add that, from the fourth century onward, the Germanic threat had significantly increased and had become a major concern in terms of state security.

I. Historical Context and the Development of the Grand Strategy of the Roman Empire

In the fifth century BCE, long before the existence of a grand defense strategy, it was the small and medium-sized landowners who were responsible for defending the Roman state, whose area of influence corresponded to barely half the surface area of the current Italian region of Lazio, i.e., an area of about 9,000 km^2. The aristocracy and those who were not proprietors (*proletarii*) were not admitted in the army, which was then seasonal. The period of military campaigns usually began in mid-March and ended in mid-October.[22]

In the second century BCE, the professional army appeared, made permanent by the continuous wars and the need to defend or pacify ever-growing territorial possessions.[23] At that time, all Roman citizens had access to the legion. Non-citizens could also enroll as auxiliary troops. The auxiliary also included foreigners or barbarians from outside the Roman world. Following his military service, the auxiliary soldier was granted Roman citizenship. This social status was highly prized at the time, as it was relatively restricted and offered many privileges. At that time, the army consisted of four legions, counting between 16,000 and 24,000 legionaries, supported by auxiliary troops which represented about a third of the number of legionaries.[24]

Already, under the Republic, these troops were subject to a strict administration and an iron discipline.[25] As one expert puts it: 'because the Romans were seldom superior in numbers or individual prowess and enjoyed only a slight advantage in technology, their capacity to maintain the cohesiveness of their units in combat often determined the outcome of a battle.'[26] During the time of the Republic, Rome began to expand its hegemony over the whole of Europe.

Arch of Septimus Severus in the Forum of Rome

This expansion was not the result of strategic planning by the heads of state. There was originally no concerted plan to conquer the known world.[27] Quite to the contrary, 'all these campaigns were waged by the Romans not so much with a view to conquering new lands as to defending their own independence and very existence (…) it was brought about by a series of incidents unforeseen, mostly unprovoked and unexpected.'[28]

The senatorial authorities issuing decrees and laws at that time did not consider the potential benefits of espionage in state affairs.[29] However, on the external scene, it was with the generals, working to extend the borders of the state by fighting the enemies of Rome, that we could find the first concrete indicators of intelligence. The senate's knowledge of external affairs was then limited to the content of the reports (*commentarii*) sent to Rome by the commander at the end of each military campaign.[30] These *commentarii* were frequently written to make the general look good rather than to report accurately on military activities that were taking place farther and farther away from the capital.[31] This was the limit of the Republican government's involvement in espionage operations. There is no historical evidence to suggest that state intelligence existed during this period. In fact, it was the emperors of a later period who would be the precursors. We will come back to this in the next chapter.

It seems reasonable to also consider that these intelligence gaps[32] could moreover be explained by the fact that the Roman state infrastructure during the Republic was limited in personnel.[33] A small state bureaucracy and a decentralized type of authority may have been unfavorable to the development of an intelligence-related infrastructure.[34] This situation began to change with the advent of the Principate.[35] With the gradual expansion of the state bureaucracy, a gradual centralization of power in the hands of the emperor and his close associates was instigated.

Thanks in large part to the combative superiority of the legions in the first century CE, Europe was already almost entirely under Roman rule. Regarding the increase in the size of the Roman army, it is proposed that as 23 CE, the frontier armies consisted of about 250,000 men, equally divided between legionaries and provincial auxiliaries.[36] The Roman Empire stretched from the Iberian Peninsula through North Africa and the Balkans to the Middle East.

At that time, static borders, called *limes*, were being developed on the limits of the Empire.[37] The Empire developed its boundaries using rivers, roads lined with forts or other types of fortifications, to protect and control its territory.[38] By the middle of the second century, the era of conquest was over, and Europe was living under the peaceful period of the *Pax Romana*. As one historian states: 'A man could work his land secure in the knowledge that a marauding band from neighboring tribes would not be permitted to carry off the results of his efforts and probably kill him and his family into the bargain. He could travel from Palmyra (Tadmur) in Syria to Eburacum (York) in north Britain without a passport and without ever feeling entirely out of place.'[39]

In terms of grand strategy, the Roman emperors were no longer working to extend the borders of the Empire but did what they could to protect what had been gained. The Empire was now at its peak. For all intents and purposes, its vastness already made it difficult to govern and defend with the means of the period. We are of course referring to the technological and material limitations of the state infrastructure of the time, such as transportation and communications. Even though the Roman infrastructure was exceptionally developed for its time, it was still limited in its role of maintaining the vast Empire. This being stated, it would erroneous to think that the scope of Roman civilization, in a general sense, was limited only to within the *limes*. There are many literary sources and archaeological records indicating that Roman influence extended far beyond the physical border of the Empire.[40]

Thus, the emperors opted for the establishment of a grand strategy of peripheral defense where the legions, which were stationed in fortresses along the fortified borders of the Empire, were tasked with repelling any armed incursion. Hence, there was no significant reserve military force stationed within the Empire. It was in that context that the intelligence role of the *frumentarii* began to be defined to provide for the internal security needs of the state. We will return to this later.

If necessary, detachments of legions could be temporarily withdrawn from one part of the secure border to support other troops stationed in a more vulnerable area. This grand strategy worked as long as enemy attacks were not repeated in a short period of time and on several fronts at once. The army's role was to provide 'continuous security for civilian life and property and insulating provincials and barbarians.'[41] Thus, in the second century, with an army of about 300,000 soldiers, the Romans were able to defend a vast empire of about 50,000,000 inhabitants living around the Mediterranean.[42]

The foundations of the grand strategy of peripheral defense can be summarized in three main points. The first was the mobility associated with the movement of troops posted on the *limes*. This mobility entitled as a 'strategic transit between the continental regions'[43] was supported by an intricate network of well-maintained roads running throughout the Empire.[44] When required, detachments of legions were temporarily withdrawn from one part of the secure border in order to support other troops in a more vulnerable area.

The second was the reluctance of Roman authorities to join to the Empire border areas that were difficult to pacify or territories for which the commitments made by the state with regard to their stewardship were considered disproportionate compared to the benefits or resources these territories provided. The state's commitments to these territories were, for example, the costs of maintaining a military presence in order to defend the region against invaders, to pacify a conquered but still hostile population, or the continuous repair of the civil and military infrastructure of these border areas under repeated attack. As for the benefits of these territories to the state, these included the fruits of agricultural production, natural resources exploitation, human resources for the army and, where urbanization was present or possible, economic opportunities and benefits.

Thus, it becomes possible to understand the reasons behind the abandonment of the Antonine Wall and the strategic retreat in favor of Hadrian's Wall in Caledonia (Scotland). Indeed, the considerable distance of the Antonine Wall from the major urban centers of Britannia (England), a land that was not conducive to large-scale agriculture, and a population that was difficult to govern are undoubtedly among the main arguments in favor of this strategic revision. With regard to the evacuation of Mesopotamia, the imperial authorities most likely concluded that the bellicose attitude of the newly conquered population, coupled with the continuing military threat posed by the Persians from the neighboring Iranian plateau, necessitated a military presence that was considered too large in exchange of the resources and income emanating from these territories. Finally, the abandonment of Dacia (Romania) was probably due, at least in part, to the fact that it had become difficult to defend because of its unfavorable geographical location. To summarize, 'Roman power could still penetrate these areas, but only at a disproportionate cost.'[45]

The third point relates to the occupation and exploitation of all territories favorable for Roman colonization and agricultural development in order to 'enhance the strength of the Empire in men and resources'[46]. In reality, the Empire was then at its maximum geographical extent. Its vastness already made it difficult to govern and defend with the means of the time. In the case of the Roman state infrastructure, even though it was extremely well developed for its time, it was still restricted in its role of maintaining the huge state apparatus that the Empire had become.

From a military point of view, following the introduction of the grand strategy of peripheral defense, there is no longer a significant military force stationed inside the Empire. With the Empire pacified, the presence of legions in the interior was no longer necessary.[47] This general context allowed the legions to remain on the *limes*.

It seems worthwhile to add that at this point the Roman were not exercising a Maginot Line approach.[48] Rather than trying to keep the frontier perfectly watertight (which seems rather simplistic, if not impractical, when the frontier is delimited by natural obstacles) the legions have the role of stemming any incursion into the territory of the Empire by carrying out limited offensives or large-scale military campaigns in enemy territory before the threat materializes on the *limes*.[49]

In the grand strategy of peripheral defense, the role of troops stationed on the *limes* was not limited to defending the border *in situ*, but rather to penetrate enemy territory and eliminate the threat before it materialized directly on the *limes*. There were two significant advantages arising from this type of operational maneuver called 'forward defense'. First, the initiative was wrested from the potential aggressor before he was in a position to attack. Second, by taking the war into enemy territory, on the *limes* fortifications, farmland and border towns of the Empire were spared from the disastrous consequences of invasion. The 'forward defense' made it possible to maintain the optimal productivity of the border areas. As we will now see, this environment changed with the advent of the grand strategy of defense in depth under the reign of Constantine I.[50]

The first signs of significant strain on the Roman peripheral defense system appeared during the reign of Marcus Aurelius (161–180), but it was during the dark period of military anarchy (235–284) that it was really tested.

Statue of Marcus Aurelius in Rome

While soldier-emperors and usurpers waged an almost continuous and merciless war to obtain the purple cloak,[51] a serious epidemic decimated the population of the Empire, and enemies from outside took advantage of the disorder to devastate the border provinces and even ventured, sometimes unopposed, deep into the heart of the Empire.[52] In addition to the Germanic and Persian incursions, the eastern provinces removed themselves from the authority of Rome, and Gaul, together with Britannia (England) and Spain, also formed an independent state.

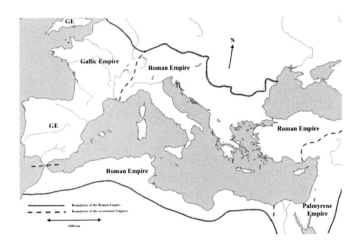

Map of the divided Empire in 260

Once order was arduously restored, the period of the Dominate began.[53]

During the reign of Constantine I (306–337), the concept of peripheral defense was abandoned for that of defense in depth.

Gold Solidus of Constantine I

This change in grand strategy of defense was probably due to the perception within the imperial circle that the borders could not be kept impenetrable, at least not at a sustainable cost. [54] It was believed at the time that determined attackers would sooner or later succeed in breaking through the defenses and then sweep into the heart of the Empire unopposed.

It is worth noting that at that time, it had become difficult to recruit Roman citizens for military service. The enrollment of foreign volunteers in the army seeking to obtain Roman citizenship greatly compensated for this shortage of recruits until the third century. But this changed with the introduction of the edict of Caracalla (211–217) in 212 (*Constitutio Antoniniana*).

Silver Antoninianus of Caracalla

Despite the many restrictions and the limited extent of its immediate impact, the edict extended access to Roman citizenship to most of the inhabitants of the Empire. This edict was not inspired by a humanitarian sentiment on behalf of the emperor but rather was driven by fiscal motivations since Roman citizens paid a special tax. In direct relevance to our study is the fact that from then on, military service was no longer the only required way for a foreigner to obtain Roman citizenship.[55] This would only aggravate the challenges associated with recruitment even though a soldier's pay had recently been increased.[56]

Until the reign of emperor Diocletian, the recruitment of Roman soldiers was conducted through a process called *dilectus.* Each recruit had to meet certain requirements that were verified during an interview (*probation*) during the recruitment process. From then on, the *dilectus* process was abandoned and landlords had to provide recruits or monetary compensation. Needless to say that they obviously did not always give the best of their peasants.

There were still volunteers, but they were few and usually and never good in times of difficulty (ruined peasants, slaves or vagabonds).[57]

By the time of the reign of Constantine I, most legionaries were Romanized foreigners or their descendants. Since the beginning of the fourth century, because of the lack of recruits, the soldier's career path was passed down from father to son by imperial decree. The profession of soldiering had become so unpopular that by the end of the fourth century, the practice of self-mutilation was widespread. Contemporary sources reported that it was common for potential recruits to cut off the thumb of one hand to prevent them from being able to bear arms.[58] Emperor Valentinian I later issued a decree stipulating that those guilty of this offense should be burned alive. But eventually, the shortage of recruits was such that this decree was rescinded and another one was put in place ordering that the mutilated would be enlisted anyway.

It is also reasonable to assume that the recent civil wars between the co-emperors of the tetrarchy for imperial supremacy (in 310, there were six co-emperors vying for this exclusive entitlement), from which Constantine I was the only one to survive, prompted him to consider the formation of a mobile army. Having learned the lessons of the recent past, Constantine I might have wanted to have a mobile army at his disposal in the heart of the Empire to deal with potential rivals, which the peripheral defense could not permit him to do. It was in that context that Constantine I set up mobile field armies.[59]

Arch of Constantine I in Rome

From that time on, the army was divided into two entities that differed in their functions. This division of the Roman army into a mobile portion positioned inside the Empire (*comitatenses*) and a static portion posted on the borders (*limitanei*) is important because it led to a multiplication of specialized units. Some of them already existed before the fourth century, but it is from that time onward that their number and diversity increased.[60]

It is worth mentioning here that some of the major fortresses of the first and second centuries on the *limes* became fortified border cities of the Empire in the fourth century. Some of them, like Vindobona (Vienna), would become the capitals of modern European nations. From that time onward, *limitanei* soldiers mingled with the population and eventually took a full part in daily urban life. Over time, the fighting capacity of these regular troops transformed into border militias deteriorated significantly.[61] As we will soon see, it was also in the fourth century that Roman intelligence activities increased, probably to partially compensate for the decline of combat capability of these *limitanei*.[62] It should also be remembered that since the mid-fourth century, while remaining a single entity, the Roman Empire was governed in two parts (East and West) to facilitate its defense and administration. Generally, there was one emperor who ruled over each sphere, sometime supported by a deputy.

Wars had become almost continuous from the fourth century onward. Consequently, regarding the general conditions of the civilian populations bordering the Empire, 'within the political and social system of the later Roman Empire, which was under considerable strain as a result of the military situation and the economic burdens imposed by it, conditions were created which might fairly be called extremely harsh.' [63]

In the second half of the fourth century, the consequences of two catastrophic military defeats signaled the beginning of the process of the decline of the *comitatenses*. The first calamity occurred at the Battle of Andrinople (Erdine) in 378, where the eastern *comitatenses* army was massacred by the Visigoths. In the battle, the eastern emperor, Valens, who attacked before the arrival of reinforcements sent by the western emperor Gratian, was killed, and two-thirds of his army, including a very large part of his infantry, were either killed or captured.[64]

Gold Solidus of Valens

Gold 1.5 Scripula of Gratian

The second military defeat with irremediable consequences was this time inflicted to the western *comitatenses* army, and ironically it was the 'restructured' eastern *comitatenses* army that was responsible. In 394, at the battle of Frigidus, the eastern emperor, Theodosius I, suffering heavy losses, inflicted a severe defeat on the western *comitatenses* army led by a usurper to the purple cloak of the West.[65] Theodosius's army, which had been reinforced with 20,000 Germanic federates,[66] reduced the usurper's army to a shadow of its former self. This military disaster for the West had similar effects to those of the defeat of Andrinople in 378 for the East. Until these bitter defeats, the Roman army of the fourth century had remained formidable, but this was no longer the case afterward.[67] Rome had suffered military defeats before, but why were these two defeats so detrimental? We mentioned earlier the difficulty of recruiting due to the unattractiveness of military service and the negative impact of the edict of Caracalla, but to fully answer that question, we must examine the medium- and long-term effects of those two factors.

Bronze Coin of Theodosius I

The losses of the *comitatenses* armies at Andrinople and Frigidus were not only of a quantitative nature, but also of a qualitative nature since it was the core of experienced veterans that had just disappeared. The core of the training of recruits relied heavily on veterans. Left with only an army weakened by heavy losses at his disposal, Valens's successor, Theodosius I, inherited the Visigoth problem, from which he could no longer rid the Empire. He was thus forced to grant them the status of federates. This type of treaty (*foedus*) had existed since the third century was to become elaborate and frequent by the early fifth century. In short, a *foedus* was a treaty of alliance between the Empire and a foreign nation recognized as an equal. In exchange for autonomous territory within the Empire and recognition of its customs, the federated nation was to provide the Empire with recruits for military service. Usually, a *foedus* was granted by the imperial authority when it was in a weak military position. In time, the *foedus* became a personal alliance between the foreign leader and a Roman Generalissimo, or the emperor himself. By the fifth century, the death of one of the parties meant the dissolution of the *foedus*, and thus of the allegiance of the federated nation to the Empire, without it renouncing the recently acquired territory. In these circumstances, the Roman authorities who were militarily vulnerable could do nothing to change this.

Theodosius I's immediate need to rebuild his army forced him to enlist entire clans of Visigoth warriors. The Visigoths were only the first of a series of Germanic nations to be recruited in this way. These contingents of federated warriors were not integrated into the Roman army but instead served in parallel. They obeyed their own leaders independently of the Roman commanders. These federated troops were not subject to the training and discipline of the Roman army and fought according to their tactics and usually with their own weapons.

These measures by Theodosius I were beneficial in the short term because he had succeeded, with the help of these additional troops, in restoring order in the East and repelling external attacks. However, the addition of large numbers of independent Germanic elements to a reduced core of Roman units had an adverse effect on the morale, training and discipline of the original core. The first symptoms soon became apparent. As soon as they were added to the eastern *comitatenses*, the Visigoths demanded monetary and additional territorial compensation for their 'loyal' services. They also became increasingly independent of imperial authority, which as we stated was unable to bring them to order by force.

This exemption from training for the federate warriors, their uncertain loyalty and the privileges they were granted infuriated their Roman counterparts. The latter were poorly paid and forced to perform unpopular civil tasks such as building and repairing roads and bridges. As a result, like the *limitanei* before them, but for different reasons, the Roman *comitatenses* gradually lost their discipline and began to increasingly shun training. It is possible that Roman commanders contributed to the neglect of training and discipline at that time by gradually putting aside those demanding concepts to limit desertions.

It would be incorrect to consider the regular entry of Germanic recruits into the Roman army, a practice that had existed since the second century, as the beginning of its 'Germanization'. The gradual recruitment of foreign elements did not pose a problem for the cohesion, discipline and fighting capacity of the army, since the recruits were Romanized and integrated into the Roman war machine.[68]

The army thus remained Roman through uniform training, even though, due to the abandonment of the military career by Roman citizens, most legionaries were foreigners or descendants of foreigners since the reign of Constantine I. The 'Germanization' of the army was rather the mass enrollment and non-integration of independent contingents of Germanic warriors, who were combined with the Roman units. This reality became apparent following the defeats of Andrinople and Frigidus. It was this 'Germanization' that had a negative impact on the morale and esprit de corps of the ever-shrinking core of Roman units.[69]

The situation was similarly detrimental in the West following the Frigidus disaster, but the difficult political climate that followed accelerated the trend toward the 'Germanization' of the Roman army. The phenomenon gained momentum because, from 406 onward, the west was prey to multiple invasions. While the east enjoyed relative tranquility on its borders, the *limes* of the west was breached in several places at once by barbarian hordes. Rome was taken and sacked in 410 by the Visigoths, who had rejected imperial authority, and was taken and sacked again in 456 by other Germanic folk, the Vandals. Once inside the Empire, some of the Barbarians were repelled, but others remained. Faced with their inevitable presence on the Empire's soil, the emperors and generalissimos of the west were forced to grant federate status to entire clans of foreign origin. Imperial authority was thus irremediably weakened by the gradual amputation of territory and resources. For instance, during the reign of emperor Honorius, the Generalissimo Constantius was forced to allow the Visigothic federates to settle in Aquitaine (418). During the reign of emperor Valentinian III, the Generalissimo Aetius was forced to do the same with the Vandals in Africa (441) and the Burgundians in Gaul (443).

Because soldiers were in short supply, the Roman authority enlisted increasingly larger contingents of federates into the army. In the west, the army, which was largely made up of federated troops of various origins, was no longer a Roman army, although it remained 'imperial'. The army with which the Generalissimo Aetius would later defeat the formidable Attila the Hun at the battle of the Catalaunian Fields in 451 was composed of Visigoths, Franks, Burgundians, Saxons, Alans and a small contingent of regular Roman soldiers who played a minor role during the battle. [70] Because the imperial army had become so heterogeneous and was directed by a loosely structured command structure, it had also become increasingly difficult to command and control. [71]

In the east, in the decades after 410, there were no immediate threats on the borders requiring numerous large-scale military campaigns. The tendency to 'Germanize' the army was therefore less predominant there and was even reversed from the reign of emperor Leo I (457–474) onward.

Gold Solidus of Leo I

Leo I had recognized the pernicious effects of the phenomenon on the army and wished to curb the growing Germanic influence on the political scene. The military climate in the east allowed the emperor to reduce the size of his army and he took advantage of this to dismiss a considerable number of Germanic federates. When a rapid influx of recruits was required, Isaurians were recruited from the mountainous regions of Cilicia (south-eastern Turkey), whose loyalty to the Empire was more secure. The period of relative peace allowed for the integration of these Isaurians, who were Roman citizens, into the Roman army, even though they had not been 'Romanized' very much until then. At the same time, within the army, there was a gradual increase in the core of Roman soldiers. The more favorable situation in the east made gradual recruitment possible as opposed to massive enrollment. As a result, training remained standardized, instilling the value of traditional troop discipline, and an increase in the fighting capacity of the army resulted. This context explains in great part why the western Empire disappeared in 476, while the eastern Empire survived the period of the great invasions of the fifth century and was able to morph into the so-called Byzantine Empire.

It was thus during the second half of the fourth century that the Roman army lost its military superiority over its enemies. In addition to hiring an ever-increasing number of mercenaries and enlisting large groups of non-Romanized Germanic warriors, the Roman authorities and generals were increasingly forced to rely on every conceivable form of diplomacy, intelligence, deception and a range of clandestine activities to ensure the survival of the regime, a role that the army was no longer able to assume by itself.[72] Except for the skill of sieges, the production of weapons and the logistical support of armies in the field, the Roman war machine had definitely lost the superiority it had over its enemies and with which it was able to adequately defend a powerful and prosperous Empire for centuries.[73]

With this context in mind, we will now address in a more concrete way the main institutional mechanisms and factors present in the Empire that were the catalysts for the development of intelligence-related activities.

II. The Catalysts for the Development of Roman Intelligence Activities and Their Agencies

As we have already stated, on the external scene, the Roman Empire was threatened on two fronts to varying degrees at different times. In the north, the Empire faced the Germanic tribes and confederations of tribes, and in the east, it had to face the Parthians and then the Persians. The defeats of Carrhae in 52 BCE and Teutberg in 9 CE showed the Romans that the Empire could not extend perpetually.[74] The Roman authorities then began to integrate the usefulness of intelligence-related activities and started to set aside their attitude of indifference toward them. [75] There were fundamental differences between the two types of threat posed by the Germanic folks and the Persians. When one assesses the disparities that existed between the two collectives in terms of administrative organization, urbanization and the level of centralization of authority, it becomes clear that the Roman authorities had to deal with two very distinct threats when collecting and exploiting intelligence.

As for the disparities in organizational structures, in addition to highlighting the absence of roads in Germanic lands, there were no large settlements, fortified towns, warehouses or weapons production centers as there were in the Empire.[76] When the Romans initiated relations with the Germanic tribes during Julius Caesar's military campaigns in Gaul around 58 BCE, bilateral trade was quickly established.[77] Through this interaction, the German folk came into contact with the prosperity of the Mediterranean world. While the Romans were content to merely trade with the Germanic tribes, the latter 'looked upon the wealth and high civilization of the Romans with a mixture of amazement and greed. Whenever we can listen to the barbarians speaking about the Roman Empire, we hear words of awe and envy.'[78] From the first contacts with the Romans, it seemed that the Germanic folk were 'drawn to the west and the south by the lure of the prestige goods economies.'[79]

During the first two centuries CE, while the art of diplomacy among the Romans was renowned for its sophistication and effectiveness, there was nothing comparable among the Germanic folk. In fact, Roman superiority in this domain was such that 'Rome manipulated the German tribes through legitimate leaders embedded within the traditional social system.'[80] In general, Roman diplomacy, inspired by the senate's motto *divide ut regnes* (divide and rule), contributed greatly to the stability of the northern frontiers until the third century.

With regard to the social organization of the Germanic tribes in the first century BCE, an extract from the *commentarii* of Julius Caesar, written during the Gallic War

(58–51 BCE), reveals a lack of interest in agriculture and animal husbandry among them.[81] Even a century and a half later, the contemporary historian Tacitus reports that arable land was only just beginning to be divided among the Germanic clans. By the second century, on the other hand, in addition to the increase in their population, the Germanic clans were firmly settled and organized, and were undergoing the 'relentless forces of cultural transformations.' [82] From then on, Roman opportunist diplomacy began to lose its effectiveness in keeping them divided.[83] In fact, it is reported that the clans who had fought against Augustus's armies had disappeared or regrouped into confederations. The most important clans: the Frisians, Chatti, the Chauci and the Alamanni confederation, which was to have a long history, appeared at the time of the reign of emperor Caracalla.[84] It is worth mentioning that from the third century onward, due to the prolonged contact with the Romans, the gap between Roman and Germanic weapons (with the exception of siege weapons) was considerably reduced.[85]

From the middle of the second century onward, invaders from the steppes of present-day Russia and Central Asia began to migrate into Eastern Europe, displacing the Germanic folk who had been established there for several generations. These peoples pushed westward and southward, in turn dislodged other Germanic groups, pushing them forward in the same direction. This domino effect on these 'increasingly mobile confederacies of warriors' [86] forced untenable pressure on the Germanic tribes settled near the *limes*. The latter, being dislodged, began to cross the limes where and when the opportunity arose. Thus, these Germanic clans who lacked land, and seeing theirs disputed by the newcomers, rushed to the *limes*, no longer to plunder the Roman provinces but to seek new lands on the other side on which to settle.[87]

The threat from the unpredictable Germanic confederations was one of constant and ever-increasing pressure on the northern border to penetrate the interior of the Empire and gain access to the riches of the civilized world. The Persian threat was of a different nature. Without dwelling too much on the complexities of the rivalry between Rome and Persia, as it would be beyond the scope of this book, suffice it to mention that it stemmed mainly from the perpetual struggle for the demarcation of the common border between the two empires and for control over Armenia.[88]

On the face of it, the Persians posed the most formidable threat to the Romans because they were a nation with the organizational infrastructure to mount major military expeditions and sustain an invasion. On the other hand, this huge state apparatus could prove to be a handicap when one considers the complexity of the preparations for such an expedition and the fact that they were difficult to conceal.[89] As for the Germanic folks, they did not have the organizational structures to sustain invasions or prolonged expeditions, but they had the advantage of the speed and unpredictability of their attacks on Roman territory.[90] Moreover, the lack of a Germanic central authority geographically located in a metropolis made it challenging for the Romans to set specific objectives in military campaigns against them. The intelligence-gathering opportunities for the Romans also differed greatly for both opponents. The sophistication of the Persian Empire's organization made it possible for ongoing and elaborate diplomatic exchanges to take place with the Romans. This increased the degree of knowledge between the potential belligerents and created opportunities in the field of espionage. For example, it became easier to detect military preparations through the presence of delegates and spies within the enemy's major cities walls. We will come back to this in the next chapter. The absence of similar conditions in the Germanic forests made these tasks much more difficult for the Romans [91] even if the considerable recruitment of Germanic soldiers in the Roman army during the Dominate provided many candidates who could convert to spies.[92]

The first catalyst for the development of intelligence-related activities was the activity of the governors of peripheral provinces. Already during the Principate, these senators (*legati*), assigned as border governors, proved to be important sources of intelligence on territories beyond the control of Rome. In addition to administering the province, maintaining justice, law and order, and managing the armies stationed in his territory, the governor also had the opportunity to gather intelligence on the border area of his responsibility. With the help of the *officium*, composed of experienced or retired military personnel, the governor prepared reports, some of which were probably intelligence-related, which he presumably kept in the archives of his residence.

We are aware of the existence of archives (*tabulae*) being kept in Rome. Already in the first century CE, the vast building once located in the Forum between the Capitol and the Arx, the *Tabularium* or 'hotel of the Archives', supposed to house since 78 BCE the official texts and documents, was no longer sufficient. We know from Suetonius that the Capitol itself contained 3,000 bronze tables that emperor Vespasian had reconstructed after the fire of '69. Various monuments and places in the imperial forums contained libraries and archives useful to the authorities and imperial administration as well as shelves of books for consultation.[93] Unfortunately, we do not actually know anything about how the 'border' reports were used during this period or how the archived documentation was used. What is emerging is that until the crisis of the mid-third century, Roman authorities did not seem to either recognize the value of pursuing external intelligence activities or perceive any threat that would justify a recourse to it.[94]

From the beginning of the fourth century, with the shift from the grand strategy of peripheral defense to the defense in depth, which led to the establishment of mobile armies, another element emerged that stimulated intelligence gathering and exploitation. The commanders of those mobile armies carried out their own intelligence gathering and exploitation, in addition to what the governors had already been doing for the previous two centuries. During this period, the governors were no longer senators (*legati*), but members of the equestrian order (*praesides*), who were military men. A new position appeared in each province, that of the commander of the border troops, called dukes (*duces*), who would have also collaborated in the exploitation of intelligence with the commander-in-chief of the armies (*magister militum*) if not the emperor himself, when he was in command of those armies. We will show examples of this occurring in the next chapter.

Continuing with the subject of foreign intelligence, we recall the contribution to intelligence-reporting made by diplomatic missions.[95] Although the primary aim of Roman diplomacy was to work to maintain the balance of power between the tribes, states and kingdoms surrounding the Roman world to avoid direct Roman military intervention as much as possible, the acquisition of intelligence is implied.[96] Clearly, diplomacy was also very useful in gathering intelligence from allies about a common enemy. We will see later that the Romans used this means to obtain information about regions not under their control, where threats to the Empire were emerging.

For Rome's allies or protectorates, it was in their interest to keep their protector informed of potential threats to their own borders.[97] Examples of this occurring are frequent. The *commentarii* of Julius Caesar, then a general, provided one that took place during the Gallic Wars.[98] As an example, Julius Caesar went on a diplomatic mission to an allied Belgian tribe, which he named Remi, to gather information about another Belgian tribe, hostile to the Romans and totally unknown to him.[99] In this way, Julius Caesar's *commentarii* brought back valuable information of a geographical, anthropological, political and economic nature on the Gallic tribes, but also on Germania, which was outside the orbit of the Roman world. Julius Caesar even learned about their way of fighting.[100] Although the *commentarii* were often written for personal political motives, they nevertheless presented clear instances of the conduct of espionage. It is important to remember that

Julius Caesar's intelligence efforts were based on personal initiatives and not on directives emanating from the republican authorities in Rome.

During the period of the Principate, Roman interventions with their allies intensified mainly because of increasing Germanic pressure on the northern border and dynastic changes among the Persians. Frequently, the emperor supported a certain claimant to the Persian crown or assisted a Germanic tribe against another, which was hostile to the Romans. This increased the opportunities for acquiring information about these regions and the people who lived there. The *Res Gestae* of Ammianus presents other concrete examples, this time from the fourth century, illustrating the exploitation of the pretext of diplomacy to spy on the Germanic folks and especially on the Persian court. The importance of diplomatic missions in Roman intelligence gathering in the fourth century will also be investigated further.

When the borders of the Roman Empire became static and militarized in the second century, hotspots of commercial and cultural exchange also developed on the periphery. These places were, in short, windows where one was necessarily brought into contact with foreign elements. Information, like people, circulated on both sides of the border through pilgrims, students, clerics, mercenaries and, above all, merchants. The markets on the *limes*, like those within the Empire, were a particularly important source of information and intelligence. [101] On the flip side, these markets could also be the origin of misinformation. In this respect, there are very few sources that refer to misinformation, but as we will see, some cases have been reported.[102]

One notion is worth mentioning before pursuing. In the collective consciousness of the Romans, memories of the achievements of the dictator Julius Caesar and the first Roman emperor Augustus were so strong that the names of both men became synonymous with distinction and poise after their deaths. Three centuries later, when Emperor Diocletian established the tetrarchy, the Empire was ruled by four co-emperors.

Silvered Bronze Antoninianus of Diocletian

Statue of the Tetrarchy in Venice

To establish the hierarchy that existed between them, the two predominant emperors took the official title of Augustus and the other two, who were in fact deputies, were designated Caesars. This explains the frequent use of these terms during the Dominate Period, as in the following incidents.

Let us now briefly discuss the role of deserters. There are many examples of Romans using information from deserters and refugees to corroborate information already in their possession. These are examples of corroboration, not absolute consideration. For example, during the last phase of the siege of Alesia in 52 BCE, Julius Caesar knew that Vercingetorix's supplies were almost depleted. This information was corroborated by deserters and prisoners long before Vercingetorix's warriors began to sacrifice old men and children by expelling them from the besieged city. [103] Four centuries later, the *Res Gestae* provides numerous examples of the Romans using information from deserters (*perfugae*) and defectors (*transfugae*).[104]

Coin of Constantius II

On the verge of undertaking a punitive military campaign against the Alamanni in 354, the Augustus Constantius II, who was located on the Gallic side of the Rhine obtained confirmation of the exact location of a shoal on the Rhine from an Alamanni deserter. Constantius II, at the head of his army, thus quickly entered enemy territory inflicting heavy losses on the dismayed Alamanni.[105]

Silver Siliqua of Julian

Three years later, Julian, then Caesar in the west (i.e., deputy to Constantius II, the sole Augustus, who nominally ruled the whole Empire at the time), had carried out a similar military campaign against the Alamanni around present-day Alsace. Julian had corroborated the information from an Alamanni deserter with the information he already possessed about the location of another shoal on the Rhine. With this information, Julian launched a successful surprise attack on the Alamanni, who had taken refuge on islands in the center of the Rhine. Using the boats abandoned by their occupants, Julian crossed the rest of the Rhine with his army to drive out the barbarians and rebuild a destroyed Roman outpost at Tres Tabernae (Salernes).[106] Once the repairs were completed, Julian pursued the Alamanni deep into their own domain. Having reached a topographically difficult region not well-known to the Romans, Julian, who was again informed by a deserter[107] learned that the Alamanni had regrouped in this area. With this information and considering that autumn was already advanced, Julian decided to turn back, realizing that pursuing the offensive would be too risky.[108]

Once the 357 campaign was over, Julian demobilized the bulk of his army, dispersing detachments along the Rhine *limes*. Julian kept only a small army with him, which he stationed at Argentoratum (Strasbourg). On learning that Julian had remained in the region and that he had only a small escort of soldiers, a coalition of seven Alamanni kinglets launched a surprise attack on the troops defending Julian.[109] The result of the battle was a Roman victory. When the dust settled, Julian was acclaimed Augustus by the enthusiastic troops. Julian, knowing that this elevation was illegitimate, declined, informing his soldiers that he did not want that honor.[110]

The *Res Gestae* also gives examples where information from deserters was exploited against the Romans. To cite just two contemporary examples with the *Res Gestae*, Ammianus reported that during the Persian siege of Amida (Diyarbakir) in 359, a siege in which Ammianus himself participated in the besieged camp, an elite Persian troop led by a Roman deserter[111] had managed to infiltrate the city through hidden tunnels under the walls. The resulting assault was repulsed, but the city eventually fell to the Persians, and Ammianus narrowly managed to escape. At about the same time, not far away, a senior Roman officer, saddled with debts, decided to join the Persians, accompanied by his entire family.[112] This officer, named Antoninus, who had learned of the dispositions and the number of Roman troops in the East, proved to be a precious assistance to the Persian king, Sapor II, during the pursuit of his offensive in Roman Mesopotamia. Sometimes the capture of enemy prisoners was joined by the successful seizure of documents. It is easy to deduce the benefits and dangers of this particular situation.[113] As for the use of geographical and ethnographical information, there is some evidence that the Romans drew up topographical maps (*itineraria*) from the Imperial Period on.[114] In general, the content of these maps was simplified, and the scale was not necessarily respected.

As for coded communication, we have also discovered indications of its use. Julius Caesar used a substitution code in which the representation of the letter was shifted by at least three spaces; for example, 'A' was replaced by 'D', 'B' by 'E' and so on. This coding system seemed to have been invented a few centuries before the time of Julius Caesar, but there is no clear written indication that it had been used before him. The *Res Gestae* also gives a concrete example of the use of coded communications by a Roman *speculatoris*, named Procopius, which we will evaluate in more detail when we discuss the master spies of the fourth century. Of this incident, it is impossible to determine whether Procopius used Caesar's alphabet or something else.[115]

Now that we are familiar with the catalysts for the development of Roman intelligence activities, let us turn to the various agencies that carried out the task of intelligence acquisition. By the end of the Republic, the Roman world had become vast, and the armies responsible for its defense were scattered around the periphery of its territory. Parallel to this territorial expansion was the construction of a road network crisscrossing the Roman world.

Artery of the Cursus Publicus

Silver Denarius of Augustus

The elaborate road system facilitated trade, troop transport and logistical support for the legions. When Augustus inaugurated the Principate in 27 BCE, he had already recognized the importance of rapid information transmission and established the Imperial Courier Service (*Cursus publicus*).[116]

The *Cursus publicus* included relays (*mansione*) where it was possible for a messenger to rest, eat and change horses.[117] The Theodosian Code of Latin Laws, written in 438, specifies that the cursus had a post office every 60–75 km and a *mansione* every 100 km.[118] The use of the *Cursus publicus* was strictly reserved for official couriers to and from the emperor, and sometimes his closest collaborators. Only the holder of a *diploma*, a permit to travel at state expense, was allowed to use the service.

In addition to facilitating the transmission of information, the *cursus* quickly became a surveillance instrument of the emperor over the population of the Empire. Augustus had an interest or at least was familiar with the benefits of the use of intelligence. In addition to considering his own military experience and the lessons learned in the civil war against Antony and Cleopatra, it is reasonable to assume that Augustus was also influenced by the intelligence-related activities described in the *commentarii* of his adoptive father Julius Caesar.

In this early Imperial Period of the Principate, a military agency (*schola*) called the *frumentarii* was responsible for the transport and distribution of grain (*frumentum*) to the soldiers of the legions stationed on the borders of the Empire. Traveling to all corners of the Roman world, the *frumentarii* acquired information about what was going on at the border and transmitted it to the emperor. Thus, a military body initially formed to ensure the supply of grain to the army developed a second role, that of an internal intelligence agency at the service of an emperor who, at the head of an increasingly centralized political apparatus, was interested in keeping informed. [119] Very quickly, the *frumentarii* became the emperor's eyes and ears for what was happening on the borders, but more so in internal affairs. The emperors employed them as law enforcers, spies, and even executioners handing down extreme sentences to the disruptive elements of the Empire's population. [120] Over time, the *frumentarii* had acquired a sinister reputation due to their unscrupulous activities and obvious signs of corruption and ended up being hated by all. [121]

At the very beginning of the fourth century, faced with growing grievances and protests, Emperor Diocletian was forced to dissolve the *frumentarii*. In a short time, Diocletian, who understood the need to maintain an intelligence *schola*, instituted a new one called *agentes in rebus*. [122] In general, the tasks of the *agentes in rebus* were derived from those of their precursors, the *frumentarii*. [123] But there were some nuances. The first was that, unlike the *frumentarii*, the *agentes* were not recruited from the military, although their hierarchical structure and titles had remained. In fact, their nomenclature in career steps followed that of the cavalry. [124] The *agentes* were instead recruited among citizens of 'good morals.' [125] Moreover, the *agentes* did not answer to the praetorian prefect, but rather to the *magister officiorum*. [126]

Since the reign of Constantine I, the *magister officiorum* was one of the four 'ministers' who were members of the consistory (*consistorium*) and formed the imperial council. These *comites* (counts) of the consistory were the emperor's closest collaborators.[127] It was from the corps of *agentes* that the *magister officiorum* recruited some of the members of his staff, which suggests that these had a certain level of education.[128] Finally, there was a considerable difference in the number of staff. While there had once been 200 *frumentarii*, the *agentes* officially numbered about 1,200.[129]

The primary role of the *agentes* was to transmit imperial directives and decrees to provincial or local authorities (letters, imperial instructions, summonses, law enforcement missions, arrests, legations, carrying of exile orders).[130] The *agentes* were also responsible for the smooth operation of the Empire's colossal administrative apparatus. Like their predecessors, they were also the supervisors and controllers of the *cursus publicus*; this included the service of horses, chariots and carriages, and the management of the *mansiones.*[131] The *agentes* were sometimes employed in the direct service of the emperor for special one-off tasks. If these missions were mainly of the nature of escorting *legati* and then *praesides* to the borders or acting as interpreters during interactions with populations located outside the Empire, [132] as we will see, they also served as spies (*speculatores*), mainly for internal affairs. [133] Like their predecessors, the *agentes* also fell into corruption and abuse of power. However, they were not disbanded since their presence was no doubt deemed indispensable by the emperors.

Regarding the sinister reputation of the *agentes*, Ammianus reported two revealing incidents. In 356, Julian, then Caesar, was conducting a customary distribution of gold to the troops to mark a holiday. When *agentes* appeared before him, they presented their open bare hands to the emperor instead of covering them with their cloaks, as was customary when receiving a largesse from the emperor. Julian, indignant but calm, is said to have declared out loud, 'it is seizing, not accepting, that the agents understand.' [134] Julian abhorred the *agentes* to such an extent that once he became Augustus and sole emperor in 361, he reduced their number to seventeen. [135] This reduction lasted only as long as his reign. Ammianus commented on another incident in which two recently dismissed *agentes* attempted to negotiate with Julian for the return of their positions and privileges in exchange for information about a colleague wanted by Julian for plotting against him. Julian did not yield to this bribe and chased them away, calling them common informants.[136]

At about the same time, the *schola* of the *agentes* was founded, the *notarii*,[137] another organization which would develop an intelligence role at the service of the emperor, was instituted. The *notarii* were not recruited from the military either, although, like the *agentes*, they adopted the military nomenclature. Like the *agentes*, this civilian body was under the direction of the *magister officiorum.* [138] Originally, the role of the *notarii* differed from that of the *agentes* in that their official role was, as clerks, to keep stenographic records of imperial audiences and of meetings of the *consistorium.* [139] As the fourth century progressed, members' profiles and roles changed. The role of the *notarii*, whose members had originally been from lowly extractions, increased from the reign of Constantine I onward and especially under Constantius II. From then on, they could rise to higher offices; they were officially constituted as a *schola*; they became militarized; and they became members of the corps of the palace's guards.[140]

Eventually, the *notarii* were asked to transmit imperial letters, orders or instructions, carry summonses, recall exiles, make arrests, conduct investigations, participate in embassies, raise recruits, carry imperial largesse and even work with military authorities in the defense of the Empire in times of war.[141] Consequently, during the third quarter of the fourth century, the distinctions between the respective roles of *agentes* and *notarii* became difficult to discern.[142] One thing was certain for both *scholae*, their activities related to law enforcement, to diplomacy in all its forms and to clandestine operations were important.[143] Moreover, their authority extended to the entire population of the Empire.

In terms of their numbers, it seems that Julian's measure of reducing the number of *agentes* also affected the *notarii*. Here again, this reduction lasted only during his reign. The number of *notarii* increased from four under Julian for the whole Empire to 125 by the year 380 in the east, and to 30 in the west by the year 444.[144] Regardless of the time period, the number of *notarii* always seemed to have remained lower than the number of *agentes*.

III. Special Operations and Foreign Intelligence in the Second Half of the Fourth Century

Except for what the *Res Gestae* tells us, we have very few details about Ammianus's life. We believe that the author of the *Res Gestae* was born in Antioch (Antakya, Turkey), around the year 330. That is the year that Rolfe, who translated Ammianus's work from Latin to English, suggests as the year of his birth. It is possible that Ammianus was born in Tyre or Sidon in Phoenicia, located in the present-day Syrian-Palestinian region. Other scholars propose a birth sometime before or in 335. The exact year of Ammianus's birth, as well as that of his death, remain uncertain.[145]

Coming from a wealthy class of society, Ammianus received an excellent education. His high social status assured him a relatively prestigious position in the army. His academic training and his military experience as a staff officer in Gaul and the eastern part of the Empire made him an invaluable witness of his time.[146] In addition to reporting in detail the political and military events of his time,

Ammianus was able to provide informed interpretations. Ammianus's account began in 353, when he was a member of the *protectores domesticus*.[147] Ammianus is thus a member of an elite corps which recruits its members in respectable families. [148] If part of Ammianus's responsibilities were administrative, as a senior staff officer, he also acquired considerable military experience, including in intelligence activities, and developed a certain ease in navigating through the political intrigues of his time.[149] In addition to forming the personal guard of the emperor, the *protectores domesticus* were frequently assigned to generals to assist them in difficult circumstances. [150] It is an assignment of this kind that Ammianus carried out in 353. In fact, he was assigned to the staff of the generalissimo Ursicinus, *magister equitum* in the east from 349 to 359.[151] During his military service with him, Ammianus was almost killed twice in combat.[152]

Modern historians recognize the *Res Gestae* as an essential source for the study of Roman history of the Dominate Period.[153] The work is even compared to the best examples of classical historiography.[154] About Ammianus's credibility and objectivity, the reviews are generally favorable. His reputation is such that he is considered as the Roman Empire's last great historian. [155] For example, Ammianus, who is not a Christian, remains unbiased about his perception of Christianity. [156] This attitude was surprising at a time when confrontations between paganism and Christianity, and even between the different Christian factions themselves, were very frequent.

Early Christian symbols in Fano, Italy

Ammianus is even presented as 'the greatest literary genius that the world has seen between Tacitus and Dante'.[157]

Ammianus's integrity is also emphasized by modern historians. The *Res Gestae* is seen as an objective work, showing reserve when presenting a more personal impression, which is uncommon for the time. [158] For example, Ammianus, who is aware of this undoubtedly distressing reality, recognized that his world was in decline. Referring to the decline of the Empire, he elegantly wrote 'and now, declining into old age, and often owing victory to its name alone, it has come to a quieter period in life'.[159] In his classic work on the decline and fall of the Roman Empire, concluding his assessment of the historical period covered by the *Res Gestae*, Gibbon writes of Ammianus: 'It is not without the most sincere regret that I must now take leave of an accurate and faithful guide, who has composed the history of his own time without indulging the prejudices and passions which usually affect the minds of a contemporary'.[160]

In addition to demonstrating a thorough knowledge of the political and military affairs of his time, Ammianus also elaborated on a variety of subjects. Without dwelling on this aspect of the *Res Gestae*, let us illustrate some examples. In 358, the city of Nicomedia (Izmit) was shaken by a violent earthquake. Ammianus, presumably in the region, undertook to describe the nature of this natural phenomenon.[161] Some of the explanations are surprisingly close to those we accept as science today, demonstrating a relatively high level of knowledge at the time. [162] Participating in Julian's Persian military campaign in 363, Ammianus offered a rather amusing explanation of the reproductive system of the palm trees that abound in the region.[163] The interpretation of the *Res Gestae* about the formation of a pearl and the explanation of an eclipse reveals Ammianus's high level of education. [164] Humor, albeit succinctly, also seems to be present. Ammianus's portrayal of the legendary bravery and impetuosity of Gallic women is revealing in this regard.[165]

During the research for this book, we found very few rather adverse comments on Ammianus's historical impartiality. Some authors question Ammianus's historical objectivity by pointing out incidents where he expressed personal perceptions and by noting gaps in his knowledge. For example, one author criticizes Ammianus (who was not a Christian) for not having a sufficient grasp of the terminology of the Christian religion. Another devotes much effort to trying to demonstrate that the philosophical perceptions expressed by Ammianus in the *Res Gestae* were not the product of independent reflection, but rather transcriptions from Neoplatonism, which was trendy at the time.[166] Another even uses arguments such as the imperfect quality of Ammianus's written Latin (who was of Greek origin) and certain inaccuracies concerning the date of certain events described in the *Res Gestae*. These arguments are of interest, but we certainly do not believe that they support the claim that presents the *Res Gestae* as a work of imaginative literature.[167] Although Ammianus sometimes revealed his opinion, we do not believe there is any reason to question his historical objectivity. For the purpose of this book, which is to evaluate the references to Roman intelligence activities, it is not important to debate Ammianus's concealed perception of Christianity or to know the exact date (March 5 or May 5) when Julian's offensive against the Persians began in 363.

When Ammianus occasionally presented rather personal perceptions, these descriptions were sufficiently attenuated and detailed enough to allow the reader to develop a more detached version of the facts. For example, when analyzing Ammianus's observations on the Roman retreat of 363, where he attempted to downplay the seriousness of the situation in which the Roman army found itself in Persia shortly after Jovian's rise, the real strategic situation became obvious because of the many details Ammianus presented during the Roman retreat. He offered details of the retreat rather than elaborate on his general opinion of the situation.[168]

Gold Solidus of Valentinian I

The immortal motto of the Roman senate *divide ut regnes* also applied to a proven intelligence practice in the fourth century.[169] It was still commonly used against the enemies of the Empire to neutralize an actual or potential external threat without the direct use of military force. For example, in 369, Valentinian I was able to neutralize an imminent threat from the Alamanni by means of a temporary alliance with a rival tribe, the Burgundians.[170] The use of special or clandestine activities was also one of the alternatives related to espionage the Romans used.[171]

Political influence activities were also observable when the Romans supported their preferred contenders for the crown of Armenia and of the Persian Empire. The case of Hormisdas was a good example of this. Hormisdas, brother of the Persian King Sapor II, had fled his homeland in around 324 and sought Roman protection. Treated with all the respect associated with his rank, Hormisdas even received the command of a large contingent of Roman cavalry from Constantius II. It was at the head of this

69

contingent that Hormisdas took part in the Persian campaign of 363 under Julian.

Without necessarily referring to the specific involvement of *speculatores*, many resource people or contacts on Rome's payroll moved incognito in foreign countries. Some circulated among the population; others were potential rulers or princes claiming the throne, while others simply moved with the inner circle of the ruling family of the targeted state. Abducting the leader of a state (or tribe) potentially hostile to the interests of the Empire was also on the list of clandestine activities employed by the Romans. For example, in 372, Valentinian I attempted to capture the Alamanni king Macrianus, who had instigated several armed incursions into Roman territory.[172] There is also evidence that the Romans exerted influence over foreign political factions, even in the form of blackmail and bribes, to destabilize a regime that was troublesome or hostile to the Roman cause. Potential pro-Roman contenders or successors were sometimes protected throughout their lives within the Empire itself.

Finally, we know that the Romans willingly engaged in political assassination operations, as in these two examples from the *Res Gestae*, where the Romans used this ploy to eliminate an external threat. In 368, on the Germanic front, Ammianus explained that Valentinian I, unable to capture the Alamanni King Vithicabius, ordered him assassinated. The gruesome endeavor was accomplished shortly after.[173]

On the Persian front, Ammianus described another example, this time instigated by Valens. In 373, the eastern emperor had decided to take the Armenian King, Papa, prisoner on suspicion of being too sympathetic to the

Persians. Valens wished to replace him with a ruler who was more favorable to the Roman cause. When Papa, who was visiting the east at the time, managed to escape and return to Armenia, Valens ordered him to be assassinated by any means necessary.[174] Not long afterward, in Armenia, Papa was murdered at a banquet. Ammianus even specifies that the murder was committed when Papa left the group with which he was feasting to answer a call of nature.[175] There is no doubt that the Romans were masters in the field of covert espionage techniques and secret missions.[176]

As we explained earlier, within the historiography related to the study of Roman intelligence, there is an ongoing debate about the importance of espionage. Some historians argue that the Romans showed little interest in espionage. The main reason behind this claim is the fact that, in order to carry out a systematic intelligence collection, there is almost no evidence to suggest that the Romans had as much interest in placing agents among neighboring populations. [177] At the other end of the spectrum of opinions, other historians argue that the significance of Roman foreign intelligence activities has been misjudged because it has simply flown under the radar.[178] We agree with the latter. We believe it would be wrong to doubt the existence of foreign intelligence activities solely based on the frequency of incidents reported by contemporary chroniclers. In addition to ignoring the importance of the limiting factors explained in Chapter One, to do so would dismiss important contextual elements. For example, on the Germanic front, one must not forget that most of the external intelligence essential to the military and civilian commanders posted on the Empire's border came from the Germanic tribes living near the *limes*. One must also remember that there were no fortified cities or centralized industries in Free Germania. These issues limited the requirements to place agents in Germanic lands. It was on the Persian front, where the Romans had to deal with a civilization as advanced as their own, that we can find more examples of placed agents. 'The *agentes* and *notarii* also sometimes served as ambassadors on important missions to foreign rulers (…) Considering that the secret agents often were involved in negotiations with foreign rulers, the usual view that their duties were primarily directed at domestic surveillance ignores the fact that when Rome needed foreign intelligence agents were available to get it.'[179]

A detailed analysis of the *Res Gestae* convincingly demonstrates that in the fourth century, the Romans were indeed involved in espionage. Ammianus reports concrete incidents of Roman espionage activities in both Germania and Persia. But before detailing these, let us summarize what we have discussed so far on intelligence-related organizations. At the time of the Republic, there was not yet an agency whose role was strictly related to intelligence. The main intelligence evidence came from the military, although it was still early to argue for the existence of an intelligence agency of its own. These activities were the result of personal initiatives on the part of border commanders or Roman generals on campaign.[180] These were not the result of pre-established directives from the authorities or of a policy integrated into the grand strategy of defense. Moreover, this type of intelligence activity seemed more tactical than strategic. In other words, these examples are more of a military reconnaissance nature than intelligence activities. Definitions may vary, but essentially, a military reconnaissance mission can be defined as an activity carried out by a military member or members, closely preceding an army on the move, to carry out observation and location on the ground. This type of activity is at the tactical level and is normally carried out during wartime.[181] At the strategic level, there is no evidence to suggest that *speculatores* were specifically engaged in foreign intelligence activities during the Republic.

We have also shown with examples of activities conducted by the *frumentarii* from the Imperial Period onward that intelligence activities were generally more frequent and varied. As we explained, at the beginning of the fourth century, the *frumentarii* were replaced by the *agentes in rebus*, and the *notarii* made their appearance. As we will see shortly, the *Res Gestae* suggests that in addition to performing internal intelligence activities, the *agentes* and the *notarii* were also called upon to perform tasks related to espionage.

Another observation must be made regarding agents engaged in foreign-intelligence activities described in the *Res Gestae*. In his work, Ammianus generally used the term *exploratores* to refer to individuals engaged in activities related to military reconnaissance. However, on rare occasions he also mentions them in a context of espionage-related activities. Both terms *speculatore* and *exploratore* are translated into English as 'scout.'[182]

The modern sources consulted are no clearer on clarifying the specific activities associated with each term.[183] It seems the two terms were more concomitant with a type of activity rather than a formal title associated to a specific organization.[184] It may be possible that in those rare cases, Ammianus was referring specifically to military personnel (*exploratores*) who were usually conducting military reconnaissance, exceptionally conducting espionage instead of the usual *agente* or *notarius* who were civilians. Alas, the available sources have not offered sufficient details to pursue this questioning without our succumbing to speculation. What is more definite is that in the fourth century, the Romans carried out espionage activities, usually conducted by agents specialized for the task and recruited among the *agentes* and the *notarii*. Those agents were usually called *speculatores*. Consequently, to lighten the text of this book, we will henceforth use the term *speculatores* to designate agents involved in espionage.

During their missions, *speculatores* did not work in groups, but rather worked covertly and alone while penetrating actual or potential hostile territory. [185] The Romans had *speculatores* working clandestinely among the people of the states or populations outside the Empire to inform the military leaders posted on the *limes* (*duci*, *praesides*) or those of the armies (*magister militum* or the emperor himself) of real or potential threats.[186]

For example, on the Germanic front, in 357 Julian had undertaken a series of military campaigns against the Alamanni and Franks that lasted three years. Following the Roman victory at Strasbourg, the Alamanni sued for peace. Peace was granted, but Julian secretly learned soon after that the Alamanni were preparing for a new offensive, with the help of reinforcements. This is how Ammianus reported the incident:

'On learning this from a sure source, Caesar (Julian) at the first quiet of nightfall embarked eight hundred soldiers on small, swift boats, so that they might go up the Rhine for a distance of twenty stadiums (3 to 4 kilometers), disembark, and with fire and sword lay waste whatever they could find.'[187]

Thanks to this military operation, the threat of the Alamanni was neutralized until the following year. It should be noted here that Ammianus used the expression 'a sure source' (*quibus clara fide compertis*) to describe the bearer of information about the Alamanni plans. Since this was a source of confirmed reliability, it could not have been a deserter or a captive. Rather, he was a *speculatore*, probably of Alamanni origin, working for the Romans. We believe that Ammianus was distinguishing between a reliable or trustworthy source and a source of unconfirmed reliability. Consistently in the *Res Gestae*, when dealing with information of unconfirmed reliability emanating from a deserter or prisoner, Ammianus retained the original designation (deserter/prisoner) even if the information obtained was corroborated or true. In other cases, when it was a source whose reliability was not in question, Ammianus used the term 'scout', the English translation of *speculatore*, (Ammianus, XXI, 13,4; XXI, 7,7; and XXV, 7,1) or expressions such as 'trusty scouts' (Ammianus, XIV, 2,15); 'tried fidelity' (Ammianus, XVII, 2,2); 'of tried loyalty' (Ammianus, XVIII, 6,2); 'trustworthy scouting party' (Ammianus, XXVII, 2,2); and 'trustworthy scout' (Ammianus, XXIX, 5,40). Ammianus frequently dissociated *speculatores* and deserters in the same statement or sentence. Here are examples of this: 'until scouts or deserters should give information of the moving of the enemy' (Ammianus,XXI,7,7); 'but the scouts and deserters who appeared from time to time' (Ammianus,XXI,13,4); 'learned from the true accounts of scouts and deserters' (Ammianus,XXV,7,2).

In 359, another case involving Julian and the Alamanni was presented by Ammianus, who explicitly demonstrated the use of a Roman *speculatore* of Germanic origin sent deep into enemy territory. After pacifying an Alamanni tribe in barbarian territory beyond the *limes*, Julian wished to learn about the intentions of another hostile tribe, this one inhabiting a region farther away from the *limes*. Let us refer directly to Ammianus:

'Without anyone's knowledge he (Julian) had sent Hariobaudes, an unattached tribune of tried fidelity and courage ostensibly as an envoy to Hortarius, a king already subdued, with the idea that he could easily go on from there to the frontiers of those against whom war was presently to be made, and find out what they were plotting; for he was thoroughly acquainted with the language of the savages (…) Hariobaudes returned after examining into everything, and reported what he had learned.'[188]

Hariobaudes may have been an *agente* or a *notarius*. But since Ammianus calls him an unattached tribune (*vacantem tribunum*), we cannot exclude the possibility that he was a soldier normally engaged in military reconnaissance activities who was asked to carry out this one-off special foreign-intelligence mission as a *speculatore*.

When we study Roman espionage activities on the Germanic front in the fourth century, we must also consider the *Arcanii*. Some modern scholars attempt to downplay their importance because there is only one historical reference to them. However, in our view, the existing evidence leaves little doubt about their presence and the nature of their activities.[189] In Book XXVIII of the *Res Gestae*, Ammianus refers to an earlier book of his, now lost, where he discussed the *Arcanii*. Let us quote this important passage:

'The *Arcanii*, a class of men established in early times, about which I said something in the history of Constans (Emperor Constans I reigned in the West from 337 to 350), had gradually become corrupted, and consequently he removed them from their post. For they were clearly convicted of having been led by the receipt, or the promise, of great booty at various times to betray to the savages what was going on among us. For it was their duty to hasten about hither and thither over long spaces, to give information to our generals of the clashes of rebellion among neighboring peoples.'[190]

Bronze Coin of Constans I

We can state without a doubt that the *Arcanii* possessed the role of monitoring the activities of the Germanic folks near the *limes* and traveled long distances outside the *limes* deep into enemy territory to gather intelligence. [191] Ammianus explains that the cause of the dissolution of the *Arcanii* was corruption. This seems plausible, considering the fate of the *frumentarii*. However, the *Arcanii* could also have been recreated in a similar form, but this does not seem to have been the case. We must then consider the possibility that the imperial authorities decided that the projected return from re-establishing this type of agency was not worth the investment of the necessary resources or the risks associated with it being reinstated. This suggests the possibility that in the fourth century, the entire responsibility for espionage was passed on to the *speculatores* recruited as needed, generally from within the *scholae* of the *agentes* and the *notarii*.

The largest number of examples of espionage activities found in the *Res Gestae* relate to Rome's difficult relation with the Persian kingdom between 358 and 363. This is largely due to the nature of the adversary. As we have already explained, the Persian Empire was a formidable opponent with whom the Romans had to deal diligently. It should be remembered that the level of social, political and especially military advancement of the Persian Empire was comparable to that of Rome. The Persians were keen to use espionage and employed various measures to counter Roman efforts in this area. Although we do have one historical reference of this type of counter measure being conducted by the Germanic folks that relates to the coercion of the *Arcanii*, we are currently not able to assert that this was a constant practice on their part.

In 357, the king of Persia, Sapor II, completed a series of military campaigns begun three years earlier against nomadic tribes that were ravaging the eastern regions of his kingdom.[192] Once the eastern borders were consolidated and the hostile tribes pacified, the territorial ambitions of Sapor II turned toward the west, on the borders with the Roman Empire. Aiming to expand his kingdom, Sapor II demanded from Emperor Constantius II the granting of the Roman provinces of Mesopotamia and Osroene, in addition to the definitive abandonment of all Roman influence on Armenia. Already in 358, with the help of rumors later confirmed by information from *speculatores*, the Romans knew the seriousness of Persian intentions. As Ammianus reports:

'The fortunes of the Orient kept sounding the dread trumpets of danger; for the king of Persia, armed with the help of the savage tribes which he had subdued, and burning with superhuman desire of extending his domain, was preparing arms, forces, and supplies (…) he planned with the first mildness of spring to overrun everything (…) news of this came, at first by rumors and then by trustworthy messengers (*nunti certi perferrent*).'[193]

The first question that comes to mind is, who were these trustworthy messengers? *Speculatores*? Persian supporters to the Roman cause? Roman or pro-Roman diplomats at the Persian court? Any of these would have been possible, but for the reasons explained above, we doubt that they were mere deserters of unconfirmed reliability or military personnel conducting military reconnaissance. Nonetheless, a series of diplomatic exchanges followed, but to no avail. Sapor II did not reduce his claims on which Constantius II could not yield. The abandonment of those strategically located provinces would have resulted in the exposure of the rest of the more difficult-to-defend Roman provinces in the east to any future Persian military aggression. Ammianus described those exchanges where it is possible to recognize espionage activity on the part of the Romans and the Persians. In connection with one of those Roman embassies sent to the Persian court, Ammianus described the intelligence activities of a *speculatore* named Procopius. As his captivating career deserves a more detailed description, we reserve this for the next chapter, which is devoted to the Roman master spies of the fourth century.

Realizing that war was probable, Constantius II left the capital of Constantinople (Istanbul) in 359 and went to Edessa (Urfa) leading a considerable army.

Egyptian obelisk in Constantinople

Ammianus reported that Constantius II remained there for a while, awaiting the return of *speculatores* sent into enemy territory to learn more about Persian preparations and movements.[194] The *Res Gestae* reported an incident in which Ammianus himself was involved in an espionage operation. Ammianus, accompanied by a centurion, went secretly to

Corduene (a mountainous region in southern Armenia, then occupied by the Persians) to inquire about events in Armenia from a supporter of the Roman cause, named Jovinianus. Ammianus and the centurion remained hidden in the mountains for three days to spy on the Persian army farther down the valley, which was preparing an invasion into Roman-held territory or Armenia.[195] Jovinianus may have been a local leader sympathetic to the Roman cause, a pro-Roman diplomat, or a *speculatore* himself.

The Romans were not the only ones to resort to intelligence activities. During Constantius II's stay in Edessa, Ammianus reported that the Persians were taking precautions in order not to divulge information that could be of interest to the Romans. Misinformation was most likely also at play.[196] Moreover, Ammianus reported that once hostilities had begun, he himself witnessed the capture and interrogation of a Persian *speculatore* of Gallic origin. Here is how Ammianus reported the event:

'There (in Meiacarire, town close to Amida) all the inhabitants had decamped, but we found one soldier hiding in a remote spot. He was brought before the general (Ursicinus) because he gave contradictory answers and so fell under suspicion. But influenced by threats made against him, he told the whole truth, saying that he was born at Paris in Gaul and served in a cavalry troop; but in fear of punishment for a fault that he had once committed he had deserted to the Persians. Then (…) he was sent as a spy (Ammianus used the term *speculatore*) to our territories and brought back trustworthy news.'[197]

Thanks to information from *speculatores*, Constantius II realized that the Persian threat was greater than expected and asked his deputy, Caesar Julian, who was fighting on the Rhine against the Alamanni, to send reinforcements.[198] It was at this point that the legions of Gaul, refusing to leave their home region, revolted and proclaimed Julian Augustus for the second time. This time, Julian could not refuse the elevation without risking assassination by his troops, to whom he had promised never to transfer out of Gaul, in exchange for their loyalty. It is worth noting that, lacking the financial resources to pay the soldiers, Julian had made this agreement to ensure the loyalty of the troops during the worst phase of the war against the Alamanni. Julian no doubt realized that this illegitimate elevation would be opposed, so he employed a *notarius* to take steps to ensure that the news did not spread too quickly. In Ammianus's words:

'Accordingly, a secretary (*notarius*) was sent to Boulogne, to watch carefully and prevent anyone from crossing the strait (English Channel). Because of this prohibition Lupicinus (a general at the head of an army fighting in northern Britannia loyal to Constantius II) returned before hearing of anything that had happened, and so could cause no disturbance.[199]'

Constantius II indeed regarded this elevation as an act of usurpation but died of natural causes in 361 before any significant opposition to Julian could materialize. From then on, Julian ruled alone over the entire Roman Empire and inherited the war against the Persians. By 362, the Persian offensive was running out of steam, and Julian decided to prepare for a counter-offensive which began the following year.[200] Ammianus, an active participant in this military campaign, described in detail the various military operations that took place. Some of them revealed

83

intelligence activities. For example, Ammianus reported that following the capture and destruction of a Persian city, a trusted informant disclosed to Julian the presence of armed troops hidden in tunnels beneath the city walls. Julian learned from this individual that the unit had planned to attack the Roman army at the first convenient moment. The Romans used fire to dislodge the ill-fated men from their hiding place; they were subsequently massacred. Again, the source was a 'trustworthy informant', and therefore a *speculatore*, not a source of unconfirmed reliability such as a deserter or a prisoner.[201]

The Roman military campaign in Persia was going relatively well until Julian was seriously injured in battle. When he succumbed due to complications, Jovian was appointed emperor to replace him.

Bronze Coin of Jovian

The Roman offensive then turned into a full-scale retreat.[202] Ammianus reported that Sapor II, whose armies had suffered heavy losses, could not take advantage of the situation, and his armed interventions were limited to harassment and scorched earth tactics against the Roman army slowly advancing toward the *limes*. Sapor II knew that the Roman army in the south was in trouble, but he also knew that there was a second Roman army stationed to the north, which was unscathed and in a position to attack. Under these circumstances, Sapor II proposed the cessation of hostilities. [203] In exchange for a reduced territorial concession from the Romans, Sapor II offered Jovian safe conduct to the border. Jovian, leading a starving and strategically disadvantaged army, accepted the peace.[204]

The Roman army in the north was too far away to directly assist Jovian, and it is reasonable to assume that he had not been in communication with it for some time. We can also assume that he was probably anxious to get to Constantinople as quickly as possible to legitimize his recent elevation. The peace was to be short-lived. It would be another generation before a more lasting peace with the Persians was to be established.[205]

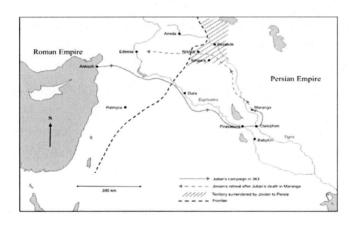

Julian's War in Persia in 363

Finally, the *Res Gestae* reported another incident of probable espionage. This time the incident took place ten years later and at the other end of the Empire. Trouble that had been developing since 365 broke into an open revolt in the western provinces of North Africa (in present-day Tunisia). The causes were the shenanigans of a corrupt governor named Romanus. In 373, Valentinian I, then emperor of the east, commissioned the able general Theodosius to depose the infamous governor, capture the rebel leader named Firmus, and finally restore order.[206] Once Theodosius arrived in Africa at the head of a considerable army, he used the services of a *speculatore* to find Firmus, who was in hiding outside of the limits of the Empire. It was with this assistance that Theodosius found Firmus. In the words of Ammianus:

'A trustworthy scout informed him that Firmus had fled to the Isaflenses (a semi-nomadic autonomous tribe living near the Sahara Desert, outside the *limes*); whereupon he invaded their lands, to demand the traitor'.[207]

Firmus was captured and executed.[208] We will discuss the origin of this revolt in the next chapter, as it implicated a corrupt *notarius*.

It has been suggested by some modern historians that the major Roman military defeats of the fourth and fifth centuries were caused by intelligence failures, the rout of Andrinople being suggested as a prime example supporting this theory. We are not convinced. Rather, we believe that the causes of the decline and ultimately the fall of the Empire in the West cannot be particularly attributed to the failure of the Roman intelligence apparatus. The existence of the Roman Empire was essentially based on its ability to defend itself militarily and to keep its enemies out of its borders. This military strength, including the projection of it, was in turn sustained by a thriving and dynamic economy. When the economic, social and political fabric of the Empire began to crumble in the fourth century, military failure became inevitable.

In a stable environment, intelligence can provide a clear advantage to the party that possesses it. But if the party is not able to take advantage of it, militarily or otherwise, intelligence becomes useless. Furthermore, we must consider the direct consequences of poor leadership, without ignoring the relative factors of luck and the presence of a particularly formidable enemy. In a brief case study to close this chapter, we will also assess the Battle of Andrinople, the event with which Ammianus ended his account in 378, to ascertain whether this Roman defeat can be attributed to an intelligence deficiency. In 376, an alarming number of Visigoths broke through the *limes* on the Danube and overflowed into the northern Balkan provinces of the Empire. The arrival of a new invader in eastern Europe, the Huns, was at the origin of this spontaneous migration. The Visigoths asked for protection within the borders of the Empire and the imperial authorities in the east agreed on the condition that they could be relied upon to defend the region against potential invaders. Once the newcomers had settled in Thrace, they were almost immediately exploited and oppressed by local officials. In 378, under the command of their leader Fritigern, the Visigoths revolted and began to ravage the region while other bands of Germanic warriors, taking advantage of the disorder, crossed the *limes* on the Danube.

Following initial military successes by local Roman troops in containing the Visigoths, the emperor of the Orient, Valens, arrived and began to organize a major counter-offensive. He had at his disposal a considerable amount of intelligence on the situation.[209] The opportunity to take the initiative arose when the Romans learned from the reports of scouts (Ammianus used here the term *speculatorum*, although these were most likely military reconnaissance operations) that the barbarians were regrouped in a defensive position in the outskirts of the city of Andrinople.[210] Some of his staff officers suggested an immediate attack, while others suggested waiting for the arrival of the army of his colleague Gratian, the emperor of the west, to make a more decisive victory possible.[211] When he arrived near the Visigoth camp, Valens saw for himself that the wagons were formed in a circle, as the scouts had stated.[212] Although this was at a tactical level, Ammianus used the terms 'careful reconnoitering' (*exploratione sollicita cognitum*) to explain the diligence with which the reconnaissance was carried out.[213] It seems that Valens was initially informed that the Visigoths numbered no more than 10,000 warriors, while he had about 20,000 soldiers under his command.[214] Valens was later informed that the numbers of Visigoth warriors were much greater, and that the enemy cavalry had not yet been located even though it was known to be in the area. With all this information in hand, Valens nevertheless decided to attack.[215]

Not long after the battle had begun, the Roman cavalry was surprised and forced off the battlefield by the Germanic cavalry that had arrived on the site. This left the bulk of the Roman army and the infantry, already engaged with the enemy, to be surrounded and unable to maneuver while being attacked from all sides. The result of the battle was an unprecedented debacle for the Romans.[216]

How to explain Valens's ultimate decision to attack before the expected reinforcements arrived? Some historians propose that Valens, who had been severely criticized in the capital for his lack of vigor toward the Visigoths since the beginning of the revolt, was forced to act quickly to restore his image with the glory associated with a military victory.[217] Others even add that it was Valens's jealousy of his nephew and emperor of the west that prompted him to attack before the arrival of reinforcements. Ammianus seems to share this view.[218] Under these circumstances, we believe it would be wrong to attribute the main responsibility for the defeat of Andrinople to a failure in Roman intelligence. Rather, we believe that the intelligence apparatus had functioned normally until the battle began. The error was then entirely related to a human factor.[219]

IV. The Pantheon of Roman Espionage in the Second Half of the Fourth Century

The detailed analysis of the *Res Gestae* presented in this book made it possible to acquire a concise chronological picture of the highlights of the careers of *speculatores* of the second half of the fourth century. While the material available is brief and generally fragmented, there is enough information to provide an overview of the activities of some of the spies of the period. Some of the intelligence activities carried out by these individuals were carried out within the borders of the Empire, while others were clearly carried out in foreign lands. It is interesting to note that while some *speculatores* had long and successful careers, others had their lives cut short by tragic means. There were also *speculatores* who abused their power, acting ignobly, while there were others who were ethical, carrying out their duties with distinction.

Notarius Paulus (353–361)

The *notarius* Paulus is the first *speculatore* presented by the *Res Gestae*. In 353, Ammianus described him as one of those among the courtiers at the court of Constantius II who

90

took advantage of the emperor's distrustful nature to secure personal gain.[220] By virtue of the title of State Secretary (*eminebat notarius*), which Ammianus used for him, Paulus was probably eminent in the hierarchy of the *notarii*. At the head of the *schola* of the *notarii*, there were three commanders (*principales*). The one at the head of the *schola* had the title of *primicerius*. His second in command was the *secundicerius*, and then came the *tertiocerius*. Paulus probably had one of those titles.[221] Ammianus reported that Paulus's reputation was such that he was sometimes called *tartareus*[222] (the diabolical) and other times *catenae* or *catenae indutum* (the chain) because he liked to degrade his captives by chaining them.[223]

In 350, the unpopular emperor of the west Constans, the younger brother of Constantius II, was overthrown in a palace conspiracy and later assassinated. Magnentius, then the commander of two legions stationed in Gaul, was acclaimed emperor of the west by the troops.

Silver 9 Siliquae of Magnentius

When Constantius II openly refused to recognize Magnentius's irregular elevation, war became inevitable. The face-off took place at Mursa, a battle from which Constantius II emerged victorious. Following a second battle with a similar outcome, Magnentius was driven to suicide.

Following Magnentius's death in 353, Constantius II gave to Paulus the task of bringing to justice the senior officers and officials who had supported Magnentius.[224] Victims of Paulus's apocalyptic zeal, those who were not condemned to die were dispossessed.[225]

In 353, while Constantius II was waging war against Magnentius in the West (351–353), he appointed Gallus as Caesar and charged him with ruling the east during his absence. Gallus was a nephew of Constantine I and half-brother of the future Emperor Julian. Gallus proved to be a cruel tyrant.[226] For example, he had many nobles in his entourage murdered for holding opinions that differed from his own. He even ordered the massacre of the entire senate of Antioch for equally derisory reasons. In 354, Gallus was arrested by the orders of Constantius II. Paulus directly participated in the trial of the close collaborators of the deposed Caesar Gallus.[227] Paulus propositioned a trial by death.[228] Gallus was put to death even before Constantius II returned from the west to participate in the proceedings. Ammianus suggested that Paulus was responsible for the hasty execution of Gallus.

In 355, Paulus also played a leading role in the trials and torture of usurper Silvanus's accomplices. General Silvanus, an infantry commander in Gaul, had supported Magnentius until the eve of the battle of Mursa, when he rallied to the cause of Constantius II. Some of Constantius II's courtiers did not forgive him this momentary lapse of loyalty. It was then that a plot was hatched in the form of a forged letter suggesting Silvanus's aspiration to the purple cloak. It seems that Silvanus was thus driven to rebellion. Following the aborted attempt to arrest Silvanus, General Ursicinus (Ammianus's superior) was sent to Gaul with the aim of defeating the usurper. Silvanus's troops were defeated at Colonia Agrippina (Cologne) and he was assassinated not long after. Ammianus explained that the forged letter had been written by an individual named Dynamius, who had used an official letter signed by Silvanus to forge another. Ammianus suggested that the scheme was probably discovered after the death of Silvanus.[229]

When Julian became sole emperor in 360, Paulus's fortune began to change. When Constantius II died the following year, Paulus lost his patron. Julian had a strong character and proved to be much less credulous than his predecessor. Moreover, as we have already shown, he had a rather unenthusiastic attitude toward *speculatores*. When Julian decided to act against the *speculatores* after numerous complaints, he reduced their numbers considerably and decided to crack down on those who had abused their authority. The *notarius* Paulus and the *agente in rebus* Apodemius (discussed below), who was also involved in the Gallus and Silvanus affairs, were among those who in turn suffered a one-sided lethal trial. This is the only clear example we found of a *notarius* and an *agente in rebus* operating together. Ammianus impassively reported the outcome of the trial as follows:

'For Apodemius, of the imperial secret service (Rolfe's translation of *enim ex agente in rebus*), who, as we have said, showed unbridled eagerness for the death of Silvanus and Gallus, was burned alive, as well as Paulus the notary (*notarium*), surnamed catena, a man to be mentioned by many with groans, who thus met the fate which was to have been hoped for.'[230]

Agente Apodemius (354–361)

The *Res Gestae* explained that an *agente* named Apodemius, accompanied by a high imperial dignitary named Barbatio, proceeded to the arrest of the deposed Caesar Gallus on the orders of Constantius II.[231] Like the *notarius* Paulus, Apodemius was also present at the trial of Gallus. We know that following the speedy trial, Gallus was beheaded.[232] It was Apodemius who personally reported the execution of Gallus to Constantius II, who was then in Mediolanum (Milan) on his way to the east, by placing the shoes of the fallen Caesar at the feet of the Augustus.[233] Apodemius also played a role in the attempted arrest of Silvanus in 355.[234] As we have shown, Apodemius's fortunes changed following the death of Constantius II. Under the orders of the new emperor Julian, Apodemius was burned alive, together with his collaborator the *notarius* Paulus.[235]

Agente in rebus then *notarius* Gaudentius (355–363)

In 355, several dignitaries and senior officers attended a social evening that took place at the residence of the governor of Second Pannonia in Sirmium (Sremke Mitrovica). Among the guests was an acquaintance of the governor, an individual named Gaudentius. He was an *agente*,[236] but the guests seemed to be unaware of this, for as the evening wore on, and no doubt because a considerable amount of wine was consumed, certain comments criticizing Constantius II's reign were articulated by some imprudent guests.[237] Ammianus then reported that Gaudentius conveyed the incident as serious. Sometime later, the authors of the statements considered disloyal were summoned to the emperor's court for trial. One of them, a man named Marinus, preferred to commit suicide rather than suffer the potential torment of a trial.[238]

In 358, Ammianus reported that Gaudentius, this time as a *notarius*, had received a mission from Constantius II to travel to Gaul to keep him informed of the actions of Julian, then Caesar. [239] In this extract, Ammianus referred to Gaudentius this time as *notarius*.[240] Although it is remotely possible that Ammianus made a mistake in confusing the two terms, which we do not believe, it is more likely that Gaudentius had simply made a switch during his career from *agente* to *notarius*. The case of Gaudentius does not seem to have been unique. Some *notarii* also came from other palatine services, such as the staff of the *magister militum* or of the *magister officiorum*; but such cases were uncommon.

When Julian was acclaimed Augustus by his troops in Gaul in 360, Constantius II sent Gaudentius to Africa to take the necessary measures to prevent that part of the Empire from submitting to Julian's authority. Here again, Ammianus designated Gaudentius as a *notarius*. [241] To understand this preventive measure on the part of Constantius II, one need only remember the importance of Africa as a source of grain for the western provinces of the Empire. The end of Gaudentius's career was just as dreadful as that of Paulus and Apodemius. In 363, Julian, now the sole ruler of the Empire, ordered that Gaudentius be arrested and executed. [242] It must have been that Julian, who we know did not think much of secret agents, did not appreciate Gaudentius's schemes conducted against him while Constantius II was still alive.

Notarius Spectatus (358–359)

As we know, in 358, the Persian King Sapor II demanded from Constantius II the concession of the Roman provinces of Mesopotamia and Osroene, in addition to the definitive abandonment of all Roman influence over Armenia. Constantius II refused any concession for reasons already explained. A series of diplomatic exchanges on both sides followed. In one of the first delegations sent by Constantius II to Sapor II, led by a Roman dignitary named Prosper, a *notarius* named Spectatus was disguised. Ammianus explains Spectatus's mission, which is a good example of espionage activity, that included finding ways to slow down the war preparations of Sapor II. [243] This statement by Ammianus is interesting because, while it is probably implied that Spectatus was to gather information from the Persian court, the intentions of the enemy ruler and the general state of war preparations, he also had the task of delaying the strengthening of the Persian defensive system on the northern borders as much as possible. We can deduce that Constantius II believed, or at least suspected, that war was imminent and that he was looking for the Achilles heel of the Persian colossus. We know nothing more about the rest of the career of this Spectatus.

Notarius Philagrius (360)

During the war he waged against the Germanic tribes on the Rhine in 360, Julian decided to capture the Alamanni king Vadomarius. Vadomarius and his warriors had been flouting Roman authority by making plundering incursions into Gaul. Julian's decision against Vadomarius was also likely influenced by the fact that a few years earlier, Vadomarius, then commander of a troop of auxiliaries, had plotted against Julian. With this objective in mind, Julian commissioned the *notarius* Philagrius to arrest Vadomarius as soon as he set foot on Roman soil. Philagrius spied on Vadomarius's movements across the *limes* into Alamanni territory, waiting for the opportunity to carry out his mission. When a banquet was organized in one of the border towns on the Rhine, Philagrius learned that Vadomarius was expected there. The *notarius* took steps to be included on the guest list. At the end of the feast, Philagrius, accompanied by some guards, proceeded to the arrest.[244] The capture of Vadomarius temporarily ended three years of war against the Alamanni.[245] Following Julian's death in 363, Vadomarius was rehabilitated. Ammianus wrote that in 365 Vadomarius was a general in Valens's eastern army, while Philagrius, in 382, was a *comes* (count) in the court of the Augustus Theodosius in the east. An interesting career progression for a *notarius*…

Notarius Decentius (360)

When Sapor II began his offensive, in 359, Constance II had a difficult time containing the invasion which was overwhelming several Roman defensive positions in the east. As we know, it was then that he decided to send a request to Caesar Julian, then warring on the Rhine against the Alamanni, requisitioning reinforcements to assist in the fight against Persians. Some historians have suggested that this measure was an attempt, on the part of a jealous

Augustus, to undermine the position of a popular Caesar with his troops and the citizens he governed. It is possible that Constantius II may have been distressed by the popularity of his deputy Julian because of his military victories and for having reduced the taxes in Gaul. However, we do not believe that this was the dominant factor in the decision of Constantius II. In our opinion, the precariousness of the Roman military situation in the east between 359 and 361 amply justified a request for reinforcements.[246] Furthermore, it would not have been in Constantius II's best interest to have Julian fail against the Alamanni and to consequently have the Alamanni overwhelm the provinces of Gaul.

To carry out this task, Constantius II sent the *notarius* Decentius to Julian.[247] As we have already indicated, the legions on the Rhine refused to leave Gaul, and proclaimed Julian Augustus. The legions and Julian remained in Gaul while Decentius returned to Constantius II without reinforcements and carrying the news concerning the elevation of Julian.[248] We know nothing more about this Decentius.

Primicerius notarius Jovianus (363)

In the summer of 363, Julian's Roman military campaign against the Persians was in full swing. Arriving in the vicinity of Ctesiphon (an ancient Persian city southeast of Baghdad, Iraq), Julian began the siege of the fortress city of Maiazomalcha (Ambar). While carrying out the attacks against the city walls, the Romans dug tunnels under the walls to reach the interior of the city. Once the tunnels were completed, simultaneous attacks were launched at several places at once to attract the defenders to the walls.[249] In due course, Ammianus reported that Roman sappers appeared inside the walls. Among the first to emerge from the breach, weapons in hand, was a tribune and *notarius* named Jovianus, who was followed by the rest of the attackers.[250] Jovianus was then *primicerius*, meaning that he held the highest position within the *schola* of the *notarii*.[251] As a *notarii*, Jovianus was a military man and probably a member of the staff of the *magister militum* Ursicinus, like Ammianus was.

The life of this courageous but imprudent *primicerius* of the *notarii* came to a sudden end shortly after the elevation of Jovian as emperor. Ammianus described the event of Jovianus enjoying a time of rest to consume an evening meal at Nisibis (Nusaybin, Turkey) as follows:

'He was taken from the dinning-table, led to a secluded spot, thrown head long into a dry well, and crushed by a great number of stones that were thrown upon him. The reason for this undoubtedly was that, after Julian's death, he too was named by a few as worthy of the throne, and that after the election of Jovian he had not acted with moderation.'[252]

Notarius Palladius (364–376)

When Valentinian I sent an army to North Africa in 373 to suppress a rebellion there, trouble had been brewing since 365. This event was discussed earlier. This delay in response was not due to negligence on the part of the imperial authorities. Rather, Valentinian I's military action was the unfortunate consequence of the activities of a corrupt *notarius*. Long before the situation in Africa degenerated into a revolt, Valentinian I had received information from merchants in Tripoli (in Libya) about financial irregularities in parts of the African provinces. Before the revolt started, Valentinian I had commissioned the *notarius* Palladius to travel to Africa to investigate the situation, under the cover of an officer responsible for distributing pay to the soldiers stationed in Tripoli.[253] Ammianus explained that, once on the scene, Palladius became the victim of a scheme and was then blackmailed by the corrupt governor, Romanus. Ammianus explained that Romanus, possibly aware of Palladius's secret mission, cleverly maneuvered Palladius into a compromising situation. As a result, Palladius was exposed to charges of embezzlement of some of the funds originally intended for the army.[254] Consequently, Palladius was coerced into falsifying his report to the emperor, declaring that everything was in order.[255]

Not long after, an envoy from Tripoli named Jovinus obtained an audience with Valentinian I to report the situation that was deteriorating in Africa. Following this meeting and unaware of Palladius's deceitfulness, Valentinian I decided to send Palladius back to investigate again, this time accompanied by Jovinus. After returning to the court, Jovinus reiterated his claims to the emperor about the ongoing disorder in Africa, confident that Palladius would corroborate his statements. When Palladius privately met the Augustus, he declared that the situation in Africa was normal and that Jovinus was the author of false assertions. Palladius's statement was supported by a letter signed by the corrupt governor Romanus. The emperor had the unfortunate Jovinus put to death for treason.[256]

It is reasonable to assume that if the situation had been properly reported to the Augustus earlier, the crisis could have been averted before it escalated into an open revolt. When the revolt finally broke out, Palladius was removed from office and forced to retire for failing to recognize the warning signs.[257] When the real causes of the rebellion were finally known and Palladius's treachery uncovered in 376, three years after the general Theodosius had brought order to Africa, Palladius was brought to justice by Emperor Gratian, son and successor of Valentinian I, who had died the previous year. Convicted of treason, Palladius hanged himself to escape the ordeal that was in store for him.[258]

Notarius Neoterius (365–390)

Shortly after the start of the troubles in North Africa in 365, a usurper was proclaimed emperor in the east, triggering a civil war in that part of the Empire. Valens, the emperor of the east, had considerable difficulty fighting this usurper named Procopius, who had a distinguished career as a *notarius* and who enjoyed considerable popularity. Procopius was so threatening that he forced the emperor in the other part of the Empire to take extraordinary measures to keep North Africa under his authority. In fact, Valentinian I feared that the forces loyal to Procopius would attempt to remove these provinces from his control in the west. One such measure was to send the *notarius* Neoterius, accompanied by two officers and a considerable troop of soldiers, to Africa with the aim of aborting any attempted invasion by means of a naval landing. We know nothing more about the career of this Neoterius except that in 390, he held the prestigious title of consul.[259] We will come back to Procopius with a detailed description of his noteworthy career.

Notarius Syagrius (369–381)

In the face of the ongoing threat from the Alamanni, Valentinian I undertook to strengthen the defensive system on the Rhine in 369. As part of this undertaking, he ordered the erection of a military outpost on the right bank of the Rhine. The work took place outside the *limes*, on the land of an allegedly pacified Alamanni clan. A group of soldiers, under the command of an officer named Arator, was appointed to carry out the work under the supervision of the *notarius* Syagrius. No sooner had the undertaking begun that the Alamanni broke the just-negotiated peace and unleashed a violent surprise attack on the soldiers engaged in construction-related labor. Ammianus reports that Syagrius was the only survivor of the attack. The emperor was furious and dismissed him.[260] We cannot comment further on the career of Syagrius except to point out that he held the dignified office of consul in 381 (under the reign of Theodosius I), which implied his eventual rehabilitation.[261]

Notarius Bassianus (371–372)

Throughout the reign of Emperor Valens in the east, the *Res Gestae* reported numerous trials related to what Ammianus describes as 'secret arts.'[262] Although to varying degrees in different periods, society's interest in esoteric practices, such as the consultation and interpretation of oracles, was a phenomenon present throughout Roman history. That said, it seems that esoteric practices were more widespread in the fourth century than in the preceding centuries.[263] It seems that Valens expressed more hostility toward this phenomenon than one could expect. Without excluding the possibility of the presence of paranoia, this hostility of Valens can also probably be explained by his strong Arian faith, as he was also notorious for his persecutions against Catholics and pagans.[264]

Some courtiers at court used this peculiarity in Valens's character to get rid of opponents or people they considered troublesome. This situation was similar to that which had existed during the reign of Constantius II, where Ammianus reported that the emperor was sometimes manipulated by unscrupulous courtiers who had economic motives behind their accusations for treason. Those who initiated these trials usually benefited from the confiscations.[265] In 371, a former *notarius* turned high official, Bassianus, was accused of attempting to 'gain foreknowledge of higher power,'[266] while his actions were interpreted as an attempt to learn the name of Valens's successor in the context of a plot. Ammianus argued that, in reality, Bassianus was attempting to find out the sex of his child, who was due to be born in the following months. Bassianus avoided a death sentence thanks to his influential family and, no doubt, the services of an eminent lawyer of the caliber of Cicero. However, Bassianus was still dispossessed of all his belongings.

Secundicerius notarius Theodore (371–372)

The case of the unfortunate *secundicerius notarius* Theodore is another example of a condemnation linked to the 'detestable arts of divination'[267] and of Valens's susceptibility. In 372, officials were sentenced to death for consulting an oracle to find out the name of Valens's successor. The result of the interpretation of the oracle's nebulous statements revealed the first four letters of the supposed name: T-H-E-O. As a result of this interpretation, a high official at Valens's court, a former *secundicerius notarius* named Theodore, was sentenced to death for allegedly aspiring to the purple cloak. [268] Some modern historians argue that Theodore was innocent. Still, others explain the condemnation by the fact that Theodore had the weakness to let himself be seduced by such a brilliant prospect, and the imprudence to maintain a compromising correspondence on this subject. [269] Ultimately, Theodore's family was dispossessed, and his wife became a court servant.

It is interesting to note the severe criticism that Ammianus attributed to Valens in Book XXIX. He wrote that some influential and unscrupulous courtiers manipulated the emperor who, in his opinion, was too gullible. [270] Many modern historians support this impression, as well as the one describing Valens as a simpleton and boorish man. [271] Ironically, the name of Valens's successor was to be Theodosius I…

Notarius Leo (371–373)

In the years 370–372, Ammianus reported that Valentinian I tried to curb corruption in Rome.

Flavian Amphitheatre (Colosseum) in Rome

As part of this effort, an investigation into an attempted poisoning of an important figure in the city was conducted by the city prefect, a man named Olybrius. The investigation progressed slowly because of the prefect's poor health. Following pressure from members of the victim's influential family, the Augustus approved the transfer of the investigation to an individual named Maximinus, who was at the same time promoted to prefect. Maximinus had until then been the governor of Etruria (a Roman province roughly corresponding to modern Tuscany, Italy) and an imperial official responsible for supplying Rome with grain. Maximinus had held these positions since 366. Ammianus added that Maximinus was an unscrupulous opportunist, waiting for the opportunity to promote himself to Valentinian I to obtain further advancement.[272] To assist him in this task and to speed up the investigation, the Augustus associated him with the *notarius* Leo. [273] Ammianus explained that once the investigation was expeditiously completed, the accused were convicted and executed. What the *Res Gestae* has retained of Leo's career is that, in 373, he held an influential office at court, and aspired to the prefecture.[274] Maximinus was later put to death in 376 by Valentinian I's successor, the Western Augustus Gratian, for abusing his authority as prefect of Rome.[275]

Trajan's column in Rome

Notarius Paternianus (374)

While engaged in a military campaign deep in Alamanni territory, Valentinian I learned in 374 that another Germanic tribe, the Quadi, had crossed the Rhine further south and broken into Roman territory. Not wishing to abandon his offensive which was in full swing, the Augustus instructed the *notarius* Paternianus to go and take stock of the situation.[276] The *Res Gestae* is silent on the rest of Paternianus's career. However, we do know that the following year Valentinian I undertook a punitive campaign against the Quadi from the military camp at Sirmium. During an audience granted to a Quadi delegation, the envoys were arrogant toward the Augustus. Enraged by this insult, Valentinian I became so angry that he succumbed to an apoplectic fit.[277]

Notarius Procopius (358–366)

Gold Solidus of Procopius

The description of the life of the *notarius* Procopius is the most detailed in the *Res Gestae* and undoubtedly the most interesting. This is partly due to his distinguished career as a *notarius*, but also because of the prominent role he played on the political scene. Procopius was born in Cilicia[278] (a region of the Empire south of modern Turkey), probably in the 320s, from a distinguished family related to the future Emperor Julian.[279] According to Ammianus, at least until the events of 365–366, Procopius's career as a *notarius* was exemplary.[280] Procopius arrived on the political scene in 358, when a series of diplomatic exchanges aimed at preserving peace between the Roman Empire and the Persian kingdom began. As we already discussed, the *notarius* Spectatus had participated in one of the first of this series of delegations. Under the pretext of making a last effort to save the peace, Constantius II sent a final delegation to Sapor II, which included the *notarius* Procopius.[281] Ammianus suggested a second motive behind Procopius's mission by relating his receipt of a coded message from Procopius while the latter was held at the Persian court.[282] Let us look at his own words:

'And when our scouts (Ammianus refers to them as *exploratoribus*) had returned there (in Amida), we found in the scabbard of a sword a parchment written in cipher, which had been brought to us by order of Procopius (…) with intentional obscurity, for fear that, if the bearers were taken and the meaning of the message known, most disastrous consequences would follow.'[283]

Ammianus was at this time located in Amida, a fortified Roman outpost in the heart of the territory claimed by Sapor II, where he supervised the reinforcement of the city's defensive system.

During Julian's reign, Procopius's career took a decisive turn. From Julian's hands, he received the honorary and prestigious title of *comes*, demonstrating his close association with the ruling family.[284] When Julian launched his military campaign against the Persians in 363, he left part of his army on the border to protect the rear of the main force, which he himself led into enemy territory. To command this army, Julian appointed General Sebastianus, to whom he joined Procopius.[285] The data on the number of soldiers varies slightly according to the sources, but Julian is said to have had a total of between 60,000 and 65,000 soldiers under his command. Between 20,000 and 25,000 soldiers would have formed the rearguard army of Sebastianus and Procopius, while the remaining 40,000 to 45,000 soldiers would have been part of Julian's offensive into Persian territory.[286] The mission of this rearguard army was to prevent Sapor II from attacking the Roman rear bases otherwise left unprotected.[287] It has also been suggested that a Roman military presence in Upper Mesopotamia was further justified because of the uncertain reliability of the Armenian King, Arsaces, who was then officially an ally but was apparently procrastinating in dispatching an armed contingent to reinforce the Roman army.[288]

Shortly after Julian's death in the middle of the campaign, Jovian was appointed emperor by the troops. The military expedition ended shortly afterward, following the ratification of what Ammianus describes as a dishonorable treaty,[289] and the wearied Roman army began a long and difficult journey back to the border. A rumor began to circulate that Julian, before the start of the 363 campaign, had instructed Procopius to assume the succession if he died in enemy territory.[290] We do not really know Procopius's intentions when he learned of Jovian's elevation. We cannot say whether he had any pretensions to the purple cloak at that time. What we do know is that Procopius decided not to do anything that could be interpreted as ambivalent and seemed to have accepted Jovian's elevation as a *fait accompli*.

Once the Roman army returned to Roman territory, Procopius was dismissed from his military duties by the perhaps suspicious Jovian, who charged him with conducting Julian's funeral in Tarsus (an ancient city near modern Adana, Turkey). [291] Procopius was most likely aware of the shenanigans going on at court against him since, following Julian's funeral, he left the public arena and was nowhere to be found.[292] It is reasonable to assume that the violent death of the *primicerius notarius* Jovianus (discussed earlier), found at the bottom of a well shortly after Jovian's ascension, may have influenced Procopius's decision to make himself *incognito*. As already mentioned, there had also been a rumor suggesting Jovianus as a contender for the purple cloak when Jovian became emperor. Ammianus added that, in order not to be recognized, Procopius even changed his physical appearance. With the help of his network of contacts, he remained informed about events and rumors circulating at court. As Ammianus put it:

'And so, after the fashion of some clever spy (*cuiusdam speculatoris*), being unrecognizable because of his unkempt appearance and leanness, he gathered the gossip, which was then becoming frequent, of many who, since men are always discontented with present conditions.'[293]

The throne became vacant again when Jovian died suddenly in 364. There are several versions of his death, but none of them refer to an assassination. Some authors suggest that Jovian was poisoned by the fumes of fresh plaster in his newly renovated room. Others suggest suffocation from the smoke of the brazier in his room. Finally, some speculate that he died of indigestion after eating too much.[294]

The competent general Valentinian I was thus promptly designated for the succession by the troops. Shortly afterward, Valentinian I elevated his own brother Valens, Augustus. Valentinian I appointed Valens to rule the East, while he reserved the West for himself. Many in the East objected to the appointment of Valens and wanted a member of the Constantinian family to return to power rather than see a new dynasty established. In addition to this opposition from supporters of the Constantinian dynasty, opposition to Valens was also due to the reaction of pagan and Catholic elements against the elevation of an Augustus who was a harsh defender of Arianism.[295] The name of Procopius began to circulate again in the capital. From his cover and aware of all that was happening in Constantinople, he worked toward obtaining the purple cloak but was waiting for the right moment to act.[296]

While Valens was fighting in Thrace to stem a Germanic incursion, Procopius returned to Constantinople and declared himself Julian's rightful successor. With the help of his supporters, who had carefully prepared for his arrival, his claim to the purple cloak was unopposed.[297] Initially only supported by the population of the capital and troops stationed nearby, the revolt spread rapidly.[298] The time to act had been carefully determined because Valentinian I, engaged in a major military campaign against the Alamanni on the Rhine, was unable to help his brother.[299] The Visigoths, on the other side of the *limes*, even offered a military support of 3,000 warriors to Procopius.

Valens decided to send two legions toward the capital with the aim of defeating the usurper. When the face-off took place, the commander of Valens's army refused to fight, instead joining forces with those he was to fight. Now pushed into the defensive, Valens fled to Ancyra (Ancara) to regroup his forces. According to Ammianus, at this point Procopius could have invaded the eastern provinces without opposition,[300] but did not seize the opportunity. Fortune changed sides as Procopius concentrated on consolidating his authority in the areas already under his control rather than pursuing Valens into Anatolia (mainland Turkey) and working to secure the loyalty of the armies posted there. It was thanks to those armies that Valens seized the initiative and launched his offensive against Procopius's disparate and smaller forces.[301] After some setbacks, Procopius's makeshift army abandoned him and joined Valens's army. Procopius tried to flee but was captured. The next day he was brought to Valens, who had him beheaded.[302] He was 40 years old.[303] To reassure Valentinian I, who had no news of his brother since the beginning of the rebellion, Valens sent him the head of Procopius, which was received with relief.[304]

Primicerius notarius Johannes (423–425)

Gold Solidus of Johannes

Our last narrative is not discussed in the *Res Gestae* since it took place about 45 years after the publication of Ammianus's work. It nevertheless is of interest because it is about the story of the interesting career of another *primicerius notarius* (thus the chief of the *schola* of the *notarii*) who also wore the purple cloak.

Nothing is known about emperor Johannes's early life other than probably being of Germanic origin and that he rose to the esteemed top job of the *notarii*.[305] He entered the political arena upon the death of Constantius III, who was co-emperor of the west with Honorius, in 421.

Gold Solidus of Constantius III

Gold Solidus of Honorius

Gold Tremissis of Valentinian III

Now a widow, Galla Placidia came into conflict with her half-brother and emperor Honorius. In 423, thanks to the efforts of Castinus, the influent advisor to Honorius, Placidia and her two children, including the future emperor Valentinian III, were banished from Ravenna, the then capital of the Western Empire. Placidia sought refuge in Constantinople. When Honorius died shortly afterward, Castinus wanted at all costs to prevent Placidia's return to Ravenna and the likelihood of her son Valentinian III being proclaimed emperor of the west. Consequently, he invested Johannes with the purple cloak in 423. Johannes knew that his ascension lacked legitimacy and immediately attempted to obtain recognition from his eastern counterpart. He had bronze and gold coins minted with his own bust and that of Theodosius II.

Gold Solidus of Theodosius II

Johannes sent emissaries to Constantinople, but they were dismissed and sent back. A new historical figure who 25 years later would play an important role on the political and military scene appeared. He was a young officer under the name of Aetius who accepted Johannes's elevation and became the director of the imperial residence. As we know, Aetius was the Roman Generalissimo who would later defeat the formidable Attila the Hun at the battle of the Catalaunian Fields in 451.

When it became clear to Johannes that Theodosius II, who had not recognized him as emperor of the west was preparing to send an army to the West to depose him in favor of the young Valentinian III, he sent Aetius to the Huns to request military assistance. The army from the East arriving by sea was led by one of Theodosius II's most competent generals, Ardaburius, assisted by his son Aspar. The campaign began badly for the forces of the east, as a storm dispersed the fleet in the Adriatic. Ardaburius's ship ran aground near Ravenna, and his crew was taken prisoner, while the rest of the fleet managed to reach and take Aquileia. Instead of taking the initiative by attacking Aquileia, Johannes preferred to wait for the arrival of Hunnic reinforcements. In the meantime, Aspar decided to attack Ravenna and, after being guided by a shepherd through the swamps surrounding the city, he entered the city without fighting. Johannes was arrested and sent to Aquileia. Johannes, whose short reign was characterized by moderation, was executed in June 425 after being mutilated and humiliated in public.

Conclusions

Roman Intelligence Service: Myth or Reality?

In this book, we have shown that during the period of the Republic, the state and military infrastructures were not compatible with the development of an intelligence service. In fact, there is currently no evidence to suggest that organized-intelligence organizations existed.[306] There were only indications of intelligence-related initiatives conducted on an individual basis. This shortfall was largely offset by a clear military and diplomatic superiority on the part of the Romans. However, this passivity relative to intelligence was gradually replaced by an ever-increasing interest in the period of the Principate. The exploitation of intelligence became more important when the superiority of Roman arms began to be challenged from the mid-second century onward. By the fourth century, the Romans had become very experienced in intelligence-related activities.[307]

During the Imperial Period, the administrative and political activities of governors (*legati*, *praesides*), the diplomatic missions to allied countries as well as to hostile territory, the observations and exchanges in the markets, and the activities of Roman commanders (*duci*, *magister militum* if not the emperor himself) were the catalysts of an environment that allowed the development of intelligence-related activities. It was in this context that domestic intelligence agencies (*frumentarii*) developed at first, followed a little later by a network of spies (*speculatores*) who resorted to clandestine operations both internally and on the foreign scene.

During the Republic, there was no central body responsible for storing and analyzing the strategic intelligence gathered. In the Imperial Period, however, the emperor had set up a permanent committee, the *consilium principis* (later called *consistorium* under Constantine I), to advise him.[308] One of its responsibilities was undoubtedly to analyze intelligence emanating from the *frumentarii* (and later *agentes in rebus*), from the *notarii* and other *speculatores* (such as the military *exploratores* and the *Arcanii*) operating outside the Empire's borders. From then on, at the intelligence level, long-term planning became a possibility.[309] However, we have no tangible evidence to confirm that this central administration body carried out permanent management of intelligence.

During the Imperial Period also appeared an agency responsible for managing the emperor's correspondence with the *legati* and then the *praesides* at the head of the provinces called *ab epistulis*. There are indications that this organization could also have been responsible for managing the reports from the *limes* drawn up by the *notarii* when a threat arose.[310] However, the traces of its activities are sporadic and not well understood.

It seems that we cannot point to a central agency whose main task was to analyze, produce, project and disseminate intelligence at the strategic level. Is it then possible to suggest that some sort of Roman intelligence service existed? Despite all the evidence indicating that the Romans were very active in intelligence-related activities and that there were agencies (*scholae*) that carried out intelligence gathering, the Romans did not appear to have set up an intelligence service in the modern sense of the term.[311]

Nonetheless, because of the nature of their activities, could the *scholae* of the *frumentarii*, the *agentes in rebus*, and the *notarii* (and even the *Arcanii*) represent an interrelated assembly worthy of consideration as an intelligence service?[312]

To further verify the rationality supporting the existence of a Roman intelligence service through these different perceptions, let us refer to the description of the simplified intelligence cycle.

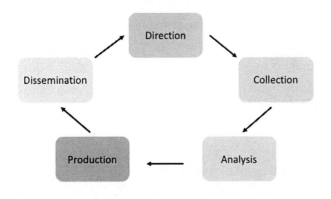

The Basic Intelligence cycle

The cycle illustrates the components and main stages of a state's intelligence apparatus.[313] There are five distinct cyclical stages that characterize the nature and operation of intelligence. The first is the needs-driven 'direction', followed by the second, which is intelligence 'gathering'. Then we have the information 'analysis' stage, which is followed by the 'production' of intelligence and finally its 'dissemination'. For the purposes of this book, we have determined that all these stages existed during the historical period under study, but nuances persisted in the optimal exploitation of the potential of some of these stages.

Let us now look at this structure in parallel with the results of our observations. When we evaluate the first stage of the cycle, which is the 'direction' given by the Roman authorities, the obvious observation is the lack of consistency and continuity. Totally absent during the Republican Period, it was only sporadic during the Imperial Period. Direction was established on an *ad hoc* basis by regional authorities and commanders. In fact, we are not aware of any clear instances where the general direction came from a central authority such as the *consistorium* or the *ab epistulis*. Direction sometimes came from the *magister militum*, the *magister officiorum*, or the emperor himself when either was in command of the armies in the field within or outside the Empire's borders. We have not discovered any historical reference suggesting the establishment of a medium- or long-term strategic plan related to intelligence on the part of the central authorities. On this point, it would be permissible to refute the existence of a centralized and permanent intelligence service among the Romans.

As we have testified, while intelligence initiatives were self-initiated and sporadic, the 'collection', and subsequently the 'analysis' phases, appear to have been more sustained. In terms of 'production' and 'dissemination', the result of the intelligence initiative went directly to the person who had initiated the cycle, either the military commander on the field or the official concerned with defeating or thwarting an internal or external threat.

Examples of this from the *Res Gestae* were abundant. Dissemination, on the other hand, was not exploited to its full potential. While the ultimate results of the intelligence did make its way into the hands of the initiator of the cycle, there does not appear to have been any indication that intelligence report storing took place in specific locations available to the central authorities for further consultation. The only possible exceptions would be when the initiator of the process was himself a member of a central authority. Consequently, we can suppose that the *consistorium* and the *ab epistulis* were the beneficiaries of the results of the intelligence cycle when the *magister militum*, the *magister officiorum*, or even when the emperor himself was leading a military campaign and was the originator of the intelligence request in the region concerned.

We can recognize that the Roman intelligence structure was not as elaborate, organized and centralized as are modern intelligence services. However, are those criteria fundamental to the definition of an intelligence service when we consider the socio-political and military realities within which the Romans operated? If the answer is yes, then we are forced to conclude that the Romans did not have an intelligence service. But if we consider the realities of life in an era long before the technological inventions that have revolutionized the world of intelligence, it may be reasonable to acknowledge that the Romans did have an intelligence service that was relevant to their needs and times.

The first element that was determined once the *Res Gestae* had been examined was that it was a fundamentally objective and reliable work. Generally, Ammianus, who demonstrated a thorough understanding of the various aspects that are integral to conducting the operations, refrained from letting his subjective beliefs overpower his narrative. [314] Incidents where Ammianus expressed a partisan or arbitrary view are sporadic and do not affect the value of the historical content of the work. In our analysis of the *Res Gestae*, while wearing an intelligence-related lens, we have maintained vigilance to manage these digressions.

Our research has shown that the *notarii*, the *agentes in rebus*, the military *exploratores* (and for a time the *Arcanii*) were employed as *speculatores* both for assignments within and outside the boundaries of the empire. In contrast, we have not discerned sufficient evidence to suggest patterns of specific assignments to either of those organizations. The *Res Gestae* seems to suggest, particularly during Julian's war with the Persians, that the *notarii* and military *exploratores* were more frequently employed than the *agentes* in tasks related to espionage. It is possible that they were more coveted by emperors than the *agentes* for this kind of missions. Unfortunately, we are unable to further verify this possible trend. We must also consider that this tendency found in the *Res Gestae* does not necessarily reflect a uniform reality throughout the Empire as well as for what took place during the rest of the fourth century and in the early fifth.

The pantheon of master spies of the second half of fourth century clearly demonstrated, with the help of concrete examples, the different roles that the *speculatores* played in Roman society. Through the abject nature of the internal activities of some *speculatores*, it became possible to conceive the reason for the unfavorable impression that people in general had of them. On the other hand, it seems that the scope of these actions was generally limited to the ruling class, affecting only a small number of the rich and influential. There were very few 'casualties' among the general population of the Empire. It is interesting to note in the *Res Gestae* that some *speculatores*, in greater numbers as *notarii*, sometimes reached very high political office. This influence in the high imperial sphere also seemed to have had its price. We need only consider the significant number of tragic demises of some of these *speculatores*.

As for questioning the existence of espionage activities among the Romans, in light of the many examples revealed by the *Res Gestae*, we believe that the Romans were indeed very active in this field. Ammianus described numerous examples of espionage operations, both among the Germanic folks and the Persians. The latter were the two main state security concerns of the Romans. For example, we need only think of the exploits of the *notarii* Philagrius and Syagrius in Germania and that of the *notarii* Spectatus, Jovianus, Procopius and Ammianus himself in Persia.

The line of thinking of some scholars today seeking to downplay or even deny the existence of espionage activities among the Romans can be explained by three factors. The first is the possible demonstration of incomplete knowledge on the part of these researchers related to the field of intelligence. Modern research into Roman intelligence activities is carried out by historians who are undoubtedly erudite, but not necessarily familiar with the idiosyncrasies, subtleties and undertones that characterize the intelligence world. This research is not generally carried out by intelligence officers, but rather is based on academic interpretations of the generally sparse, fragmentary and sometimes equivocal historical information available. This factor could lead to misinterpretations of the meaning of certain events and actions and to the difficulties in unscrambling activities that are associated with espionage from those related to military reconnaissance.

For example, one modern author designates as a 'reconnaissance mission' Ammianus's pre-war foreign intelligence assignment when, accompanied by a centurion, he went clandestinely to Corduene to find out about events in Armenia from a supporter of the Roman cause.[315] As we have stated earlier, we know that a military reconnaissance mission is an activity carried out by one or more military personnel, preceding an army on the move by some normally short distance, who carry out observation and location on the ground. Military reconnaissance is conducted at the tactical level and is normally carried out during wartime. This type of activity differs greatly from a peacetime foreign intelligence mission, during which a senior staff officer accompanied by a senior 'non-commissioned' officer infiltrates deep into foreign territory to secretly meet with a source of known reliability to gather intelligence on a potential enemy's activities.

The same can be argued about Procopius's clandestine pre-war mission at the Persian court epitomized by the coded message hidden in a sword's scabbard he secretly sent back to Roman authorities. Moreover, although we have only one historical reference to them, the description of the activities conducted by the *Arcanii* were very different from those associated with military reconnaissance. Even if sometimes espionage missions were conducted by military personnel (*exploratores*), they were nevertheless espionage missions, not merely reconnaissance operations.

And what to say about the special operations described in the *Res Gestae*? Whether it was the kidnapping of the Alamanni King Vadomarius in 360, the assassination of the Alamanni King Vithicabius in 368, the attempted kidnapping of the Alamanni King Macrianus in 372, or the assassination of the Armenian King Papa in 373, all those examples demonstrate the presence of undercover Roman agents operating in foreign lands as spies to find targeted individuals. Furthermore, considering that part of the tasks of both the *agentes* and *notarii* were also to apply imperial sanctioned sentences (law enforcement missions, making arrests, executioners applying extreme punishments), we believe that the *speculatores* who were tasked to find those kidnaping or assassination targets in foreign lands and those who executed/applied those imperial sentences when the targets were located and identified were probably the same individuals. Here again, we believe that none of those activities can reasonably be defined solely as military reconnaissance activities.

The second factor is related to the translation of Latin terms related to intelligence. It is possible that some ambiguous translations are the cause of inadequate modern interpretations of certain Latin terms used by fourth-century authors. We need only consider, for example, Ammianus's use of the terms *speculatore* and *exploratore* without apparent distinction (both translated as 'scout' in English) to refer to agents involved in activities related to military reconnaissance and others engaged in foreign intelligence activities. Only with a thorough interpretation of the text discussing each representation of these terms can one distinguish which of the two activities Ammianus is referring to. To highlight just one example of a recent limited interpretation of the term *speculatores* in a specialized publication, the author, who mentions the term *speculatores* only once, translates the term as 'scouts' without further explanation or possible reference to intelligence.[316]

Another example of ambiguity is the translation of the term *notarius*. The English translation of this term is 'secretary' or 'stenographer'. An uninformed reader can easily be misled by the limited modern meaning of these terms. As we have determined, in addition to the initial administrative tasks of the *notarii*, there were also intelligence-related activities, sometimes carried out outside the boundaries of the Roman Empire. In the *Res Gestae*, Ammianus used this term on the assumption that the reader was familiar with its contemporary meaning. Unless this was explained in one of his previous 13 books that were lost, Ammianus did not consider it necessary to provide precise and detailed explanations. In fact, it was only by analyzing the very activities of the people, which the Ammianus calls *notarii*, that it became possible to determine the real nature and extent of their activities.

Finally, the third factor is the lack of available contemporary sources on foreign intelligence. Because of the very small number of sources, the possibilities for comparison or corroboration are limited. In short, there are not enough reported cases of Roman espionage activities to convince some researchers of their existence.

At the beginning of this book, we outlined the main difficulties associated with the study of Roman intelligence. One of these was the Roman desire to conceal intelligence activities because they were seen as unworthy and contrary to the Roman warrior tradition. Considering what we have just demonstrated, a question comes to mind. Is it possible that the ambiguity surrounding the definitions of the terms *speculatore* and *notarius* were the indication of a desire on the part of the classical Roman authors to conceal the presence of espionage activities? We cannot exclude this possibility. Indeed, it may also explain, at least in part, the abolition of the *Arcanii* and the absence of an official Roman intelligence service.

Roman arms

In light of what we have demonstrated in this book, we can confidently state that the Romans of the Imperial Period were active in the field of intelligence and that the fourth century represented its 'golden age'. As for the contested recognition of the existence of Roman espionage activities, we would simply have to disagree.

Chronology of Main Events

27 BCE	Augustus becomes emperor.
	Beginning of the Imperial Period.
98–117	Reign of Trajan.
CE	End of the period of great military conquests.
	Beginning of the period of the *Pax romana*.
117–138	Reign of Hadrian.
	Establishment of the Grand Strategy of Peripheral Defense.
161–180	Reign of Marcus Aurelius.
180	Advent of Commodus.
	End of the *Pax romana*.
235–284	Military anarchy and Germanic migrations: Empire in crisis.
284–305	Reign of Diocletian.
293–306	The Tetrarchy.
330	Approximate birth of Ammianus Marcellinus in Antioch, Syria.
306–337	Reign of Constantine I.
	Establishment of the Grand Strategy of Defense in Depth.
337	Death of Constantine I, known as the Great, sole Augustus of the Roman Empire.

	Constantine II, Constantius II and Constant; sons of Constantine I reign in association.
340	Death of Constantine II.
350	Death of Constant, Constantius II, sole Augustus of the Roman Empire.
	Probable beginning of Ammianus's military career.
	Usurpation of Magnentius in the west.
351	Constantius Gallus appointed Caesar and deputy to Constantius II.
353	Ammianus assigned to the staff of Ursicinus, commander of the army in the East.
	Defeat and death of Magnentius.
	Beginning of the historical period covered by *Res Gestae*.
354	Trial and death of Caesar Constantius Gallus.
	Persians at war with nomads on their eastern borders (354–357).
355	Silvanus acclaimed Augustus in the west by his troops.
	Ursicinus defeats Silvanus at Colonia Agrippinensis (Cologne).
	Death of Silvanus.
	Constantius II appoints Julian Caesar who assists him in ruling the west.
357	Ursicinus and Ammianus leave Gaul for the East.
	Julian's military campaigns in Gaul against the Alamanni and Franks (357–360).

	Julian acclaimed Augustus by his troops following the victory at Strasbourg. Julian declines.
358	Beginning of the Persian offensive in Armenia and Roman Mesopotamia.
359	Beginning of Constantius II's war against the Persians in the East (359–363).
	Siege and fall of Amida to the Persians.
360	Ammianus in Antioch and disgrace of Ursicinus.
	Julian again acclaimed Augustus in the west by his troops. Julian accepts.
	Important Roman cities in the east taken by the Persians.
361	Death of Constantius II, Julian alone Augustus.
363	Julian's military campaign against the Persians.
	Death of Julian succeeded by Jovian.
	End of the war against the Persians.
	Retreat and territorial concessions by the Romans.
	Return of Ammianus to Antioch, probable end of his military career.
	Beginning of Ammianus's work on the *Res Gestae*.
364	Death of Jovian; Valentinian I succeed him as Augustus.
	Valens elevated to Augustus of the East by Valentinian I, Augustus of the West.

365	Revolt in North Africa due to the abuses and corruption of the governor Romanus.
	War of Valentinian I against the Alamanni (365–372).
	Usurpation of Procopius in the east.
368	War against the Persians who tried to annex Armenia, independent since 363.
373	Revolt in North Africa suppressed.
	War of Valentinian I against the Alamanni and the Quadi (373–375).
375	Death of Valentinian I. His son Gratian succeeds him as Augustus in the west.
378	Battle of Andrinople: Roman defeat and death of Valens.
	End of the historical period covered by the *Res Gestae*.
380	Ammianus begins writing the *Res Gestae*.
390	Publication of the *Res Gestae*.
394	Battle of Frigidus.
379–395	Reign of Theodosius I, who reigned alone from 383 to 395.
	Beginning of the 'Germanization' of the Roman army.
395–423	Reign of Honorius in the west.
	Final division of the Empire.
	Multiple Germanic invasions in the west.
425–455	Reign of Valentinian III in the west.
457–474	Reign of Leo I in the east.
	Reversal of the 'Germanization' in the east.
476	Fall of the Empire in the west.

Glossary

Arianism   doctrine representing Jesus as the son of God without being of the same nature as his father, thus denying the divinity of Christ

Brazier   metal vessel containing burning coal used for heating

Comes   Latin term for 'companion' which became a secular title granted to trusted officials of the emperor during the Dominate

Commentari   reports or accounts sent to Rome by a commander at the end of each military campaign

Dominate   phase of the Roman Empire corresponding to the period from the reign of Diocletian in 284 CE to the fall of the Western Roman Empire in 476 CE. It is considered as more authoritarian, more bureaucratic and less collaborative than the previous Principate period.

Limes   fortified borders of the Roman Empire with no natural defenses

Pax romana	century between the reign of Trajan (98–177) and that of Severus Alexander (222–235), which corresponds to the apogee of Roman civilization
Principate	phase of the Roman Empire corresponding to the period from the reign of Augustus in 27 BCE to the advent of the reign of Diocletian in 284 CE. This period is characterized by the reign of a single emperor (or princeps) and is aimed at preserving the illusion of continuity of the Republic
Purple cloak	garment, sheet dyed purple and symbol of authority; dignity of consuls and other sovereign magistrates under the Republic; designation of the emperor under the imperial regime
Republic	period of classical Roman history that began in 509 BCE and lasted until the rise of the Empire in 27 BCE
Res Gestae	historical work written at the end of the 4th century by Ammianus Marcellinus, considered an essential source for the study of the Roman history of the Dominate
Tetrarchy	system of government where authority is shared between four emperors. In addition to facilitating the management of the Empire, this system was also an attempt to rationalize the succession process by

avoiding the emergence of usurpers and internal armed conflicts.

List of Illustrations

Rome's architectural treasures, Front cover (Photograph of the author)

The author, Back cover (Photograph from the author)

Portico of the Library of Celsus in Ephesus, Turkey, p. 19 (Photograph from the author)

Arch of Septimius Severus in the Forum of Rome, p.22 (Photograph from the author)

Statue of Marcus Aurelius in Rome, p.29 (Photograph from the author)

'Map of the divided Empire in 260, p.30 (Illustration from the author with base map provided by https://d-maps.com/carte.php?num_car=2228&lang=en)'.

Gold Solidus of Constantine I, p.31 (With permission of wildwinds.com, ex Numismatica Ars Classica)

Silver Antoninianus of Caracalla, p.32 (Courtesy of Chip Gruszczinski)

Arch of Constantine I in Rome, p.34 (Photograph from the author)

Gold Solidus of Valens, p.36 (With permission of wildwinds.com, ex CNG Coins and Triton Auctions)

Gold 1.5 Scripula of Gratian, p.36 (With permission of wildwinds.com)

Bronze coin of Theodosius I, p.37 (Private collection)

Gold Solidus of Leo I, p.42 (With permission of wildwinds.com, ex Freeman & Sear and Gemini Auctions)

Silvered Bronze Antoninianus of Diocletian, p.52 (Courtesy of Chip Gruszczinski)

Statue of the Tetrarchy in Venice with the author in proximity, p.53 (Photograph from the author)

Coin of Constantius II, p.54 (Private collection)

Silver Siliqua of Julian, p.55 (Courtesy of Chip Gruszczinski)

Artery of the Cursus publicus, p.58 (Photograph from the author)

Christian symbols in Fano, Italy, p.66 (Photograph from the author)

Silver Denarius of Augustus, p.58 (With permission of wildwinds.com, ex Freeman & Sear and Gemini Auctions)

Gold Solidus of Valentinian I, p.69 (Courtesy of Chip Gruszczinski)

Bronze coin of Constans, p.77 (Courtesy of Chip Gruszczinski)

Egyptian obelisk in Constantinople, p.81 (Photograph from the author)

Bronze coin of Jovian, p.84 (Courtesy of Chip Gruszczinski)

'Map of Julian's war in Persia in 363, p.85 (Illustration from the author with base map provided by https://d-maps.com/carte.php?num_car=2228&lang=en)

Silver 9 Siliquae coin of Magnentius, p.91 (With permission of wildwinds.com, ex Numismatica Ars Classica)

Flavian Amphitheater (Colosseum) in Rome, p.104 (Photograph from the author)

Trajan's column in Rome, p. 106 (Photograph from the author)

Gold Solidus of Procopius, p.107 (With permission of wildwinds.com, ex Numismatica Ars Classica)

Gold Solidus of Johannes, p.113 (With permission of wildwinds.com, ex CNG Coins and Triton Auctions)

Gold Solidus of Constantius III, p.114 (With permission of wildwinds.com, ex CNG Coins and Triton Auctions)

Gold Solidus of Honorius, p.114 (With permission of wildwinds.com, ex CNG Coins and Triton Auctions)

Gold Tremissis of Valentinian III, p. 114 (Courtesy of Chip Gruszczinski)

Gold Solidus of Theodosius II, p.115 (With permission of wildwinds.com, ex CNG Coins and Triton Auctions)

Graph of the Intelligence cycle, p.119 (Graph from the author)

Roman arms, p.140 (Photograph from the author)

Bibliography

Ammianus Marcellinus (1935) *Res Gestae*, translation J.C. Rolfe, volume I (books 14 to 19), Cambridge, Loeb Classical Library, 583p.

Ammianus Marcellinus (1940) *Res Gestae*, translation J.C. Rolfe, volume II (books 20 to 26), Cambridge, Loeb Classical Library, 683p.

Ammianus Marcellinus (1939) *Res Gestae*, translation J.C. Rolfe, volume III (books 27 to 31), Cambridge, Loeb Classical Library, 602p.

Ardant Du Picq C. (1978) *Études sur le combat. Combat antique et combat moderne*, Paris, Éditions Champ Libre, 236p.

Austin N. (1979) *Ammianus on Warfare: An Investigation into Ammianus' Military Knowledge*, coll. Latomus, vol. 165, Bruxelles, Revue d'études latines.

Austin N. and Rankov N. (1995) *Exploratio: Military and Political Intelligence in the Roman World from the Second Punic War to the Battle of Adrianople*, London, Routledge.

Balard M. (1990) *Le Moyen Âge en Occident,* Hachette Supérieur, Paris.

Baldelli G. Paci, E. Tomassini L. (1994) *La Battaglia del Metauro, Testi, Tesi, Ipotesi*, Fano, Italia, Minardi Editore.

Barnes T.D. (1998) *Ammianus Marcellinus and the Representation of Historical Reality*, Ithaca, New York, Cornell University Press.

Bartolini M. (2023) *Roman Emperors A guide to the Men who Ruled the Empire*, Barnsley, Pen & Sword Books Limited.

Bartolini M. (2007) 'L'espion devenu empereur : Procope d'après Ammien Marcellin', *Histoire Antique*, Éditions Faton, France, 31.

Bartolini M. (2004) 'Ammien Marcellin et le renseignement extérieur romain', *Scripta Mediterranea*, University of Toronto, XXIV.

Bartolini M. *Apport stratégique au déclin de l'armée romaine : la grande stratégie de défense en profondeur*, « Histoire Antique », Éditions Harnois, Part I, No.12, (Décembre 2003–Janvier 2004), pp.58–65; Part II, No.13, (Février-Mars 2004).

Bartolini M. (2003) 'Les causes du changement de la grande stratégie romaine de défense périphérique à la défense en profondeur au IIIe siècle', *Ancient History Bulletin*, 17.3–4.

Besnier M. (1937) *L'Empire romain de l'avènement des Sévères au Concile de Nicée*, Paris, Presses Universitaires de France.

Bey F. (Novembre-Décembre 2001) *À la croisée des chemins. L'armée romaine de 117 à 217 ap. J.-C.*, « Ordre de Bataille », no 41.

Blockley R.C. (1975) *Ammianus Marcellinus: A Study of his Historiography and Political Thought*, coll. Latomus, vol. 141, Bruxelles, Revues d'études latines.

Brauer G.C. (1975) *The Age of the Soldier Emperors. Imperial Rome 244–284*, New Jersey, Noyes Press.

Bunson M. (1991) *A Dictionary of the Roman Empire*, New York, Oxford University Press.

Bunson M. (1994) *Encyclopaedia of the Roman Empire*, New York, Facts On File.

Carl L. (1996) *CIA Insider's Dictionary*, Washington D.C., NIBC, Press.

Chaliand G. (1990) *Anthologie mondiale de la stratégie*, Paris, Robert Laffont.

Chevalier R Et Poignault R. (1998) *L'empereur Hadrien, « Que sais-je? »*, Presses Universitaires de France.

Constans L.A. (1981) *Guerre des Gaules*, Paris, Gallimard.

Coumert M Et Dumézil B. (2020) *Les royaumes barbares en Occident, « Que sais-je? »*, Presses Universitaires de France.

Crump G. (1975) *Ammianus Marcellinus as a Military Historian*, Wiesbaden, Franz Steiner Verlag GMBH.

CUNLIFFE B. *Greeks, Romans and Barbarians Sphere of Interaction*, London, B.T. Batsford Ltd., 1988.

Dautremer L. (1899) *Ammien Marcellin*, « Études d'histoire littéraire », tome VII, Lille, Presses universitaires de Lille.

Dearth D.H. and Goodden R.T. (1995) *Strategic Intelligence: Theory and Application*, Washington, DIA, PA17013–5050, Second Edition.

Delmaire R. (1995) *Les institutions du Bas-Empire de Constantin à Justinien*, Paris, Les Éditions du Cerf.

Drijvers J.W. and Hunt D. (1999) *The Late Roman World and its Historian: Interpreting Ammianus Marcellinus*, New York, Routledge.

Dvornik F. (1974) *Origins of Intelligence Services*, New Brunswick, N.J., Rutgers University Press.

143

Ferrill A. (1991) *Roman Imperial Grand Strategy*, Lantham, University Press of America.

Ferrill A. (1998) *The Fall of the Roman Empire. The Military Explanation*, London, Thames and Hudson Ltd.

Forty S. (2019) *Roman Soldier: Operations Manual*, Sparkford, Hynes Publishing.

Gaddis J.L. (Winter 1987/88) 'Containment and the Logic of Strategy', *The National Interest*, 10.

Gariel A. (1939) *Dictionnaire Latin-Français*, collection Portefeuille, Librairie Hatier, Paris.

Garnsey P. and Saller R. (1987) *The Roman Empire: Economy, Society, Culture*, London.

Gibbon E. *The Decline and Fall of the Roman Empire*, tome 2, Toronto, Alfred A. Knopf, 1993 (original 1929).

Gibbon E. *The Decline and Fall of the Roman Empire*, tome 3, Toronto, Alfred A. Knopf, 1993 (original 1929).

Goldsworthy A. (2000) *Roman Warfare*, London, Cassell & Co.

Hacquard G. (1952) *Guide romain antique*, Paris, Hachette.

Hanne W.G. (January-March 1982) *Ethics in Intelligence*, 'Military Intelligence', no. 1.

Ind A. (1963) *A Short History of Espionage*, New York, David McKay.

Isaac B. (1990) *The Limits of Empire: The Roman Army in the East*, Oxford.

Jomini A.H. (1977) Précis de l'art de la guerre, Paris, Éditions Champ Libre.

Jones A. (1964) *The Later Roman Empire*, vol 2, Oxford, Blackwell.

Kahn D. (1996) *The Code Breakers*, New York, Scribner.

Kennedy P. (1987) *The Rise and Fall of the Great Powers*, New York, Random House.

Krizan L. (1999) 'Intelligence Essentials for Everyone', *Occasional Paper Number Six*, Washington D.C., Joint Military Intelligence College.

Lee A. (1993) *Information and Frontiers. Roman Foreign Relations in Late Antiquity*, Cambridge, Cambridge University Press.

Le Bohec Y. (2021) *Histoire de la Rome antique, « Que sais-je? »*, Presses Universitaires de France.

Le Roux P. *L'Empire romain, « Que sais-je? »*, Presses Universitaires de France, 2022.

Luttwak E. (1979) *The Grand Strategy of the Roman Empire*, Baltimore, The John Hopkins University Press.

Macdowall S. and Embleton G. (1994) 'Late Roman Infantryman 236–565 A.D.', *Warrior Series*, 9, Osprey Publishing.

Macdowall S. and Hook C. (1995) *Late Roman Cavalryman 236–565 A.D.*, Warrior Series, no 15, Osprey Publishing.

Macmullen R. (1976) *Roman Government's Response to Crisis. A.D. 235–337*, New Haven, Yale University Press.

Magie D. (1950) *Roman Rule in Asia Minor*, Princeton, Princeton University Press, vol 1.

Mengel M. and Murphy D. (April 2001) 'A Rural Lycian Bath House, Abstract', *American Journal of Archaeology*, 105, 2.

Millar F. (1982) 'Emperors, Frontiers and Foreign Relations 31B.C.-A.D.378', *Britannia*, 13.

Neilson K. and Mckercher B. (1992) *Go Spy the Land, Military Intelligence in History*, Westport, Connecticut, Praeger.

O'Flynn J.M. (1983) *Generalissimos of the Western Roman Empire*, Edmonton, The University of Alberta Press.

Paret P. (1986) *Makers of Modern Strategy,* Princeton University Press, New Jersey.

Petit P. (1974) *La crise de l'Empire 161–284*, coll. Histoire générale de l'Empire romain, tome 2, Paris, Éditions du Seuil.

Piekalkiewicz J. (1988) *World History of Espionage: Agents, Systems, Operations*, Washington, D.C., National Intelligence Book Center.

Public Affairs Staff. (1994) *A Consumer's Guide to Intelligence*, Washington, PAS94–00039.

Rémy B. (1998) *Dioclétien et la tétrarchie, « Que sais-je? »*, Presses Universitaires de France.

Schmidt J. (2018) *Le déclin de l'Empire romain, « Que sais-je? »,* Presses Universitaires de France.

Scott T. (Autumn 1999) *On Roman Military Intelligence*, 'Criminal Intelligence', no 4.

Sheldon R. (Fall 1997) 'The Ancient Imperative: Clandestine Operations and Covert Action', *International Journal of Intelligence and Counterintelligence*, 10, 3.

Sheldon R. (Spring 1993) 'The Spartacus Rebellion: A Roman Intelligence Failure*?*', International Journal of Intelligence and Counterintelligence, 6, 1.

Sheldon R. (1987) *Tinker, Tailor, Caesar, Spy: Espionage in Ancient Rome*, (Ph.D. thesis), University of Michigan, Ann Arbor, Michigan.

Simkins M. and Youens M. (1974) *The Roman Army from Caesar to Trajan*, Berkshire, Osprey Publishing Ltd.

Sinnigen W. *Origins of the Frumentarii*, 'Memoirs of the American Academy in Rome', 1962.

Sinnigen W. (1961) 'Two Branches of the Late Roman Secret Service', *American Journal of Philology*, 80.

Southern P. and Dixon K. (1996) *The late Roman Army*, New Haven, Yale University Press.

Syme R. (1968) *Ammianus and the Historia Augusta*, Oxford, Clarendon Press.

Thompson E.A. (1982) *Romans and Barbarians. The Decline of the Western Empire*, Wisconsin, The University of Wisconsin Press.

Todd M. (1987) *The Northern Barbarians 1000 BC–AD 300*, Oxford, Basil Blackwell Ltd.

Wells C. (1984) *The Roman Empire*, Glasgow, William Collins Sons & Co. Ltd.

Wheeler E.L. (January 1993) 'Methodological Limits and Mirage of Roman Strategy: Part I', *The Journal of Military History*, 57.

Wheeler E.L. (April 1993) 'Methodological Limits and Mirage of Roman Strategy: Part II', *The Journal of Military History*, 57.

Wheeler E.L. (1988) *Stratagem and the Vocabulary of Military Trickery*, Leiden, E.J. Brill.

Whittaker C.R. (1994) *Frontiers of the Roman Empire*, Baltimore, John Hopkins University Press.

Windrow M. and Mcbride A. (1996) *Imperial Rome at War*, Hong Kong, Concord Publications Co.

WISEMAN J. (November/December 2000) 'Barbarians at the Gate', *Archaeology*, 53, 6.

Web links cited

https://en.wikipedia.org/wiki/Reconnaissance
Oxford Languages

https://www.dictionary.com/browse/reconnaissance

https://www.merriam-webster.com/dictionary/reconnaissance

End Notes

[1] As a definition of grand strategy, we propose the following which describes it as being 'the integration of a state's overall political, economic, and military aims, both in peace and war, to preserve long-term interests, including the management of ends and means, diplomacy, and national morale and political culture in both the military and civilian spheres' (Wheeler E.L. (January 1993) 'Methodological Limits and Mirage of Roman Strategy: Part I', *The Journal of Military History*, 57, p.10).

[2] Isaac B. The Limits of Empire: The Roman Army in the East, Oxford, 1990 is an example of this.

[3] Wheeler E.L. (April 1993) 'Methodological Limits and Mirage of Roman Strategy: Part II', *The Journal of Military History*, 57, p.216.

[4] Ferrill A. (1991) *Roman Imperial Grand Strategy, Lantham*, University Press of America. The Republic was the period of classical Roman history that began in 509 BCE and lasted until the rise of the Empire in 27 BCE.

[5] Wheeler, *Op. Cit.,* Part II, p.229–230.

[6] Lee A. (1993) *Information and Frontiers. Roman Foreign Relations in Late Antiquity*, Cambridge, Cambridge

University Press, p.xi.

[7] Crump G. (1975) *Ammianus Marcellinus as a Military Historian*, Wiesbaden, Franz Steiner Verlag GMBH, p.1–2.

[8] Sheldon R. (1987) *Tinker, Tailor, Caesar, Spy: Espionage in Ancient Rome*, (Ph.D. thesis), University of Michigan, Ann Arbor, Michigan, p.X.

[9] Krizan L. (1999) 'Intelligence Essentials for Everyone', *Occasional Paper Number Six*, Washington, D.C., Joint Military Intelligence College, p.7.

[10] Carl L. (1996) *CIA Insider's Dictionary*, Washington D.C., NIBC, Press, p.281.

[11] *Ibid.*, p.281

[12] Hanne W.G. (January-March 1982) 'Ethics in Intelligence', *Military Intelligence*, 1.

[13] Lee. *Op. Cit.,* p.150.

[14] Austin N. and Rankov N. (1995) *Exploratio: Military and Political Intelligence in the Roman World from the Second Punic War to the Battle of Adrianople*, London, Routledge, p.9.

[15] Sheldon R.M. (Fall 1997) 'The Ancient Imperative: Clandestine Operations and Covert Action', *International Journal of Intelligence and Counterintelligence*, 10, 3, p.299–315.

[16] The Parthians are referred to as Persians from 224 CE because of a major dynastic change. The core of the Persian kingdom then corresponds to the present territory of Iran and Iraq.

[17] Drijvers J.W. and Hunt D. (1999) *The Late Roman World and its Historian: Interpreting Ammianus Marcellinus*, New York, Routledge, p.195.

[18] Dvornik strongly supports this military and diplomatic

superiority of the Romans until the fourth century (Dvornik F. (1974) *Origins of Intelligence Services*, New Brunswick, N.J., Rutgers University Press, p.53–54).

[19] Sheldon. *The Ancient Imperative…*, p.300.

[20] Wheeler E. (1988) *Stratagem and the Vocabulary of Military Trickery*, Leiden, E.J. Brill, p.X.

[21] Sheldon. *Tinker, Tailor…*, p.1.

[22] As Merivale suggests: 'the Roman legions were a militia enrolled practically for home service only'; Merivale C. (1887) *The Roman Triumvirates*, New York, Charles Scribners's Sons, p.8.

[23] As a champion of the plebs, general Caius Marius gathered around him the dissatisfied and the under-represented of society. After a career as a magistrate, he became consul in 107 BCE. Marius carried out a major reform of the army by admitting the previously excluded poor. The later gradually replaced the peasants and the owners in the legion, thus making it a professional army. This army, which was now entirely devoted to its leader, changed the balance of power between the Senate and the army. Indeed, this new political reality, where senatorial authority was reduced, was a prelude to the gradual process of the advent of the Empire in 27 BCE. The military successes of Marius against the Berbers and Germanic tribes led the Senate to appoint him proconsul in 105 BCE. The aristocracy, injured by the reforms of Marius in favour of the plebs, had its own representative in the person of Lucius Cornelius Sulla. This very ambitious character took advantage of a turnaround favourable to the aristocracy to supersede Marius and take his place as the dominant figure on the political scene.

[24] Hacquard G. (1952) *Guide romain antique*, Paris, Hachette, p.64.

[25] Jomini A.H. (1977) *Précis de l'art de la guerre*, Paris, Éditions Champ Libre, p.71.

[26] Crump G. (1975) *Ammianus Marcellinus as a Military Historian*, Wiesbaden, Franz Steiner Verlag GMBH, p.83.

[27] Le Roux P. (2022) *L'Empire romain, « Que sais-je? »*, Presses Universitaires de France, p.9.

[28] Dvornik. *Op. Cit.,* p.50–52. Piekalkiewicz shares this view by stating that 'the Romans in their first military expeditions were less concerned with the conquest of countries than with securing their independence and their own existence' (Piekalkiewicz J. (1988) *World History of Espionage: Agents, Systems, Operations*, Washington, D.C., National Intelligence Book Center, p.83). Austin also adds that 'it was ignorance, not knowledge of the world which she tried to conquer that was most characteristic of Republican Rome' (Austin N. et Rankov N. (1995) *Exploratio: Military and Political Intelligence in the Roman World from the Second Punic War to the Battle of Adrianople*, London, Routledge, p.108). 'Aussi étonnant que le fait puisse paraître, Rome a souvent été contrainte au conflit; ses habitants aimaient la paix, détestaient la guerre. Mais quand il fallait la faire, ils la faisaient, et ils ne s'arrêtaient qu'à la victoire (…) Entre 509 et 338, des guerres incessantes menacèrent la Ville presque en permanence. Les Étrusques voulaient reprendre une ville perdue (guerre de Porsenna en 508 ou 507; guerre contre Véies de 406 à 396) et les voisins, Sabins au nord-est, Èques à l'est (458) et Volsques au sud, voulaient la piller en même temps détruire un ennemi militairement dangereux. Une

guerre contre les Latins prit place dès 499 (ou 496). En 390, des Gaulois, qui s'étaient installés dans la plaine du Pô, s'ajoutèrent aux autres pillards; ils revinrent en 367. (…) Le besoin de sécurité sans doute poussa les Romains à de dure guerres contre les Samnites, dans des montagnes d'accès difficile. La tradition énumère trois guerres samnites, en 343–341, 326–304 et 298–290. Puis les Campaniens et les Latins s'unirent contre les Romains. La ligue latine attaqua de 340 à 380 mais, à la fin, elle fut battue.' (Le Bohec Y. (2021) *Histoire de la Rome antique, « Que sais-je? »*, Presses Universitaires de France, p.3–14)

[29] 'During the days of the Republic, however, the Roman government took no steps to organize an institutional network for gaining knowledge of other governments' political and military plans' insists Ferrill (Neilson. *Op. Cit.,* p.17).

[30] Austin explains that 'Roman commanders in the field were normally given a free hand during a campaign (…) However, it was usual for them, at least at the end of a campaigning season, to send dispatches to Rome'. (Austin. *Exploratio…*p.95).

[31] These *commentarii* were often written for personal political motives and presented the general under an attractive light rather than to inform (Austin. *Exploratio…*p.89).

[32] Or should we instead say the non-recognition of the utility of intelligence in the affairs of the State…About this, Scott specifies that 'intelligence must be recognized as a concept that was fully understood by the Romans in its importance, but it was not fully implemented by those responsible' (Scott T. (Autumn 1999) 'On Roman Military Intelligence', *Criminal Intelligence*, 4, p.3).

[33] This is what Garnsey and Saller call a *'government without bureaucracy'* (Garnsey P. and Saller R. (1987) *The Roman Empire: Economy, Society, Culture*, London).

[34] On this point, Austin adds that 'no such mission (related to intelligence) is known to have been ordered by the Republican Senate, which is hardly surprising in view of its annual magistracies and intense political rivalries which made long-term strategic planning virtually impossible (…) the Senate itself had no permanent officials or standing committees, its executive officers being those same magistrates whose annual election was seen as a principal safeguard of the constitution' (Austin. *Exploratio…*p.30 and 87).

[35] 'The emergence of this level of bureaucracy appears to have begun with the early Principate (…) Relatively small numbers of office staff would be required to look after these documents' specifies Austin (Austin. *Exploratio…*, p.161). Ferrill adds 'the Romans did eventually develop an intelligence network in the imperial regime, and by the late first century A.D. it had become an institutionalized branch of the government' (Neilson. *Op. Cit.*, p.18).

[36] Wiseman J. (November/December 2000) 'Barbarians at the Gate', *Archaeology*, 53, 6, p.13.

[37] As a general definition of the term *limes*, we refer to the fortified frontier of the Empire, which includes natural or geographical boundaries. Wiseman adds that 'the frontier was marked in a variety of ways, sometimes incorporating natural features (rivers and mountains), but invariably including military stations connected by a network of roads' (Wiseman J. (November/December 2000) 'Barbarians at the Gate', *Archaeology*, 53, 6, p.13).

[38] Austin, *Exploratio...,* p.111.

[39] Simkins M. et Youens M. (1974) *The Roman Army from Caesar to Trajan*, Berkshire, Osprey Publishing Ltd., p.40.

[40] For more details on this, consult Whittaker C.R. (1994) *Frontiers of the Roman Empire*, Baltimore, John Hopkins University Press.

[41] Luttwak, Op. Cit., p.78.

[42] Ferrill. A. (1988) *The Fall of the Roman Empire. The Military Explanation*, London, Thames and Hudson Ltd., p.26. Other estimates suggest an army composed of a number between 315,000 and 350,000 legionaries plus auxiliaries (Chevalier R Et Poignault R. (1998) *L'empereur Hadrien, « Que sais-je? »,* Presses Universitaires de France, p.59) and a total population of up to 80 million (Le Roux, *Op. Cit.*, p.55).

[43] Luttwak, *Op. Cit.*, p.96.

[44] Regarding the speed of travel on Roman roads, Ferrill states that this system was 'as rapid as it could be without benefit of nineteenth and twentieth-century means of electronic transmissions, on average about fifty miles per day'; Ferrill, Roman Imperial..., *Op Cit.*, p.18.

[45] Luttwak, *Op. Cit.,* p.46.

[46] Luttwak, *Op. Cit.*, p.96.

[47] Ferrill adds 'cohesive economically and politically, Romans were thus released from the need to maintain internal security by force'; Ferrill, Roman Imperial..., *Op. Cit.*, p.19.

[48] Wheeler, *Op. Cit.,* Part I, p.25.

[49] Ferrill, Roman Imperial..., *Op Cit.*, p.22. 'During this phase of empire, the operational method of border defence against high-intensity threats was mobile and offensive, not

static: combat was to take place beyond the border rather than within it'; Luttwak, *Op. Cit.*, p.66.

[50] For more information, with supporting schematics on '*forward defence*' consult Luttwak E. (1979) *The Grand Strategy of the Roman Empire*, Baltimore, The John Hopkins University Press, p.61 to 145; Ferrill. *The Fall...*, p.25 to 50; Bartolini, M. (Décembre 2003–Janvier 2004), *Apport stratégique au déclin de l'armée romaine : la grande stratégie de défense en profondeur*, Histoire Antique, Éditions Harnois, Part I, No.12, (pp.58–65; Part II, No.13), (Février-Mars 2004), pp. 64–67; and Bartolini, M. (2003) *Les causes du changement de la grande stratégie romaine de défense périphérique à la défense en profondeur au IIIe siècle*, Ancient History Bulletin, 17.3–4, pp.195–212.

[51] During this troubled period, which lasted almost fifty years, more than twenty emperors succeeded one another, not counting an equal number of usurpers.

[52] Between 165 and 270, two major pandemics decimated the population of the Empire. The Antonine plague which began in 165 and lasted until 190 was the first known pandemic impacting the Roman Empire. The total death count has been estimated between five and ten million, roughly 10 percent of the population of the Empire. Lucius Verus, co-emperor with Marcus Aurelius, fell victim of it. (Bartolini M. (2023) *Roman Emperors: A Guide to the Men Who Rules the Empire*, Pen & Sword Books, p.31). The Cyprian plague emerged in 251 and infected the population of the Empire until 270. There are no historical accounts comprehensive enough to estimate the total number of deaths of the Cyprian plague in the Roman Empire;

however, its impact was likely as significant as the Antonine plague. Emperor Claudius Gothicus (268–270) fell victim to it. Both plagues are estimated to have caused widespread manpower shortages for food production and for the Roman army, severely weakening the Empire during the military anarchy crisis. (Coumert. M, Dumézil B. (2020) *Les royaumes barbares en Occident, « Que sais-je? »*, Presses Universitaires de France, p.35).

[53] On the subject of the period of the Dominate, Hunt points out that it is during this period that imperial authority took on the appearance of monarchy. The court adopted a 'heightened sense of self-importance cocooned in an exaggerated language and ceremonial of majestic isolation, protected at close quarters by serried ranks of flattering courtiers, and further afield by a comprehensive network of state security' (Drijvers. *Op. Cit.*, p.53). It is in this context that the golden age of Roman intelligence began. We will return to this in subsequent chapters.

[54] Ferrill. *The Fall...*, p.45. This is what Gaddis calls an asymmetric grand strategy. He states that 'in a general sense, all strategies are either symmetrical ones which seek to minimise the risk to 'national' security or asymmetrical ones which accept greater risk in exchange for lower costs' (Gaddis J.L. (Winter 1987/88) 'Containment and the Logic of Strategy', *The National Interest*, 10, p.29–31).

[55] To this effect, Gibbon adds that 'it was much easier to obtain the pecuniary contributions than the military service of the subjects of the Empire' (Gibbon. *The Decline...*, tome 2, p.222). For additional details, see Bartolini. *Roman Emperors Op. Cit.* p.41–43.

[56] Forty S. (2019) *Roman Soldier: Operations Manual*,

Sparkford, Hynes Publishing, p.67.

[57] Le Bohec. *Op, Cit.*, p.108.

[58] Ammianus,XV,12,3.

[59] Ferrill. *The Fall*...p.43. Crump adds that this 'new system of defence was designed to make the armies more flexible in their reactions' (Crump. *Op. Cit.*, p.46).

[60] For example, the mounted archers (Sagitarii), the pikemen (Lanciarii) and the rear-guard commandos (*Superventores*) (Ferrill. *The Fall*..., p.78).

[61] Ferrill, *The Fall*...p.25 to 50.

[62] Austin explains that 'amongst the periods of Roman history for which we have good evidence, that covered by Ammianus appears as a high-water mark of Roman strategic intelligence'. (Austin. *Exploratio*..., p.241). It was during this period that real intelligence-related predispositions at the borders emerged which would allow earlier and better warning of any threat which might materialize. (*Ibid.,* p.185).

[63] Blockley. *Op. Cit.,* p.104.

[64] Windrow M. and Mcbride A. (1996) *Imperial Rome at War*. Hong Kong, Concord Publications, p.42.

[65] This usurper, Eugene, was a professor of Latin and rhetoric who had become a senior civil servant. According to Delmaire, Eugene had been a *magister scriniorum* (Delmaire R. (1995) *Les institutions du Bas-Empire de Constantin à Justinien*, Paris, Les Éditions du Cerf, p.68). The latter was raised to the purple cloak by the *magister militum* of the West, Argobast. At that time, Argobast was the real authority in the west and opposed the claims of Theodosius I to the west.

[66] Ferrill. *The Fall*..., p.84.

[67] Southern. *Op. Cit.*, p.39.

[68] 'L'intégration de 'barbares' dans l'armée de campagne semble anachronique au IIIe siècle. (…) On évitera de parler prématurément de 'germanisation' de l'armée romaine dont le contenu doit être, de toute façon, analysé et nuancé' Le Roux. *Op. Cit.*, p.116.

[69] Following the defeats of Andrinople and Frigidus, there was a chronic lack of candidates for recruitment. Soldiers were passed down from father to son by imperial decree and Germanic federates were enrolled in the Roman army *en masse*. As Crump states, 'the foederati were of course used from the beginning of the fourth century, but the majority of Germanic warriors in imperial service were enrolled as individuals in Roman units or in strictly controlled contingents of *laeti* and *gentiles*. The first extensive use of federate troops came under Theodosius' (Crump. *Op. Cit.*, p.66).

[70] In 451, Attila crossed the Upper Danube and entered Gaul, where Aetius was waiting for him with a cosmopolitan army of Visigoths, Alans, Franks and Romans. Despite the death in battle of Theodoric I, King of the Visigoths (not to be confused with the future king of the Ostrogoths, 493–526, of the same name, who will also mark history), the battle of the Catalaunian Fields was a decisive victory for Aetius. It was the only military setback Attila would suffer.

[71] By the fifth century, 'L'armée romaine a perdu sa cohésion, d'autant que, pour combler la perte de ses effectifs, elle incorpore des mercenaires qui ne sont pas Romains et constituent souvent comme une cinquième colonne.' (Schmidt J. (2018) *Le déclin de l'Empire romain,*

« *Que sais-je*? », Presses Universitaires de France, p.114).

[72] As an example, O'Flynn states that 'this concern with maintaining a delicate balance of barbarian forces reflects the degree of Rome's weakness at this time; she survived, as has often been remarked, by playing off one lot of barbarians against another' (O' Flynn J.M. (1983) *Generalissimos of the Western Roman Empire*, Edmonton, The University of Alberta Press, p.98).

[73] On this point, Goldsworthy explains that 'by the fourth century the Roman army found itself more often as the defender than the attacker in siege operations and had developed the skill of defence to a high art' (Goldsworthy A. (2000) *Roman Warfare*, London, Cassell & Co., p.191).

[74] The crushing defeat of Carrhae 'showed that attacking the Parthians head-on was neither the most successful nor most efficient policy (…) Since force of arms did not seem to work, the next governor of Syria (…) turned to covert activity (…) The return of the standards was accomplished (30 years later), not through military means, but through clandestine bartering, kidnapping and blackmail that went on behind the scenes' (Sheldon. *The Ancient Imperative…*, p.302–306). Similarly, the annihilation of three Roman legions at the Battle of Teutberg convinced Emperor Augustus that it was probably impossible to conquer all of Germania. These two traditional enemies of Rome would persist throughout the history of the Empire. In the fourth century Crump adds that 'in Ammianus' time the military strength of Rome faced a growing challenge from both her traditional enemies (Crump. *Op. Cit.*, p.46).

[75] Scott. *Op. Cit.*, p.1. Lee adds that 'the ability of the empire to cope with these changed circumstances was

affected in part by its access to reliable information and intelligence about those neighbours' (Lee. *Op. Cit.,* p.III).

[76] Lee. *Op. cit.,* p.89 to 158; Neilson. *Op. Cit.,* p.25.

[77] For the Romans, 'the north had much to offer: amber, wild animals for the beast shows, furs, cattle and hides, and slaves'; Cunliffe B. (1988) *Greeks, Romans and Barbarians Sphere of Interaction*, London, B.T. Batsford Ltd., p.182.

[78] Thompson E.A. (1982) *Romans and Barbarians. The Decline of the Western Empire*, Wisconsin, The University of Wisconsin Press, p.3.

[79] Cunliffe, *Op. Cit.*, p.189.

[80] Cunliffe, *Op. Cit.*, p.183.

[81] Cunliffe, *Op. Cit.*, p.175.

[82] Luttwak, *Op. Cit.*, p.193.

[83] Cunliffe, *Op. Cit.*, p.183.

[84] Petit P. (1974) *La crise de l'Empire 161–284, coll. Histoire générale de l'Empire romain*, tome 2, Paris, Éditions du Seuil, p.140.

[85] Todd M. (1987) *The Northern Barbarians 1000 BC–AD 300*, Oxford, Basil Blackwell Ltd., p.155–191.

[86] Cunliffe, *Op. Cit.*, p.191.

[87] Petit, *Op. Cit.*, p.26.

[88] On this, Goldsworthy states that 'conflicts between the two powers had tended to focus on domination of the areas between their frontiers, especially the kingdom of Armenia' (Goldsworthy. *Op. Cit.*, p.183). As for Armenia, Sheldon adds that 'neither Rome or Parthia could allow the other to occupy it without loss of security and prestige' (Sheldon. *The Ancient Imperative...*, p. 301).

[89] As Barnes specifies, 'strategic surprise, in the sense of mounting an unexpected invasion against an unprepared

foe, was impossible in ancient conditions' (Barnes. *Op. Cit.*, p.163).

[90] 'The threat on the Danubian and the Rhine sectors was permanent. The Parthian threat, on the other hand, was sporadic; Rome's eastern wars, being fought with an organized state, had a beginning and an end' (Luttwak. *Op. Cit.,* p.145).

[91] 'It has become apparent that a variety of circumstances increased the availability of information in the east compared to the north' (Lee. *Op. Cit.,* p.183).

[92] Bartolini M. (2004) 'Ammien Marcellin et le renseignement extérieur romain', *Scripta Mediterranea*, University of Toronto, Volume XXIV, 2004, p.7

[93] Le Roux. *Op. Cit.*, p.44.

[94] 'Les empereurs, avant les guerres du IIIe siècle, recevaient des ambassades venues de tous les horizons, sans exclusivité, semble-t-il. Les marchands, les prisonniers libérés pouvaient apporter des renseignements. Tout se passe comme si Rome en avait conclu que le danger n'était pas sérieux'. (Le Roux. *Op. Cit.*, p.113.)

[95] Austin states that 'the value of diplomatic operations of this nature for the acquisition of important strategic intelligence cannot be overestimated' (Austin. *Exploratio...,* p.19). Lee adds that 'in the context of information-gathering, embassies could also make a major contribution in this area' (Lee. *Op. Cit.,* p.166).

[96] Luttwak. *Op. Cit.,* p.31.

[97] Austin. *Exploratio...,* p.89. Sheldon adds that 'wherever Rome established its presence, pro-Roman parties came to power and thereafter supplied intelligence as needed' (Sheldon. *Tinker, Tailor...,* p.59).

[98] Julius Caesar organized for the first time in Roman history a regular information service by messenger on horseback (Dvornik. *Op. Cit.,* p.86). Piekalkiewicz adds that Julius Caesar 'attained great military success not only through his extraordinary talents as field commander but also because he attributed appropriate significance to the role of spies' (Piekalkiewicz. *Op. Cit.,* p.97).

[99] Constans L.A. (1981) *Guerre des Gaules,* Paris, Gallimard, p.100).

[100] In this regard, Austin claims that Julius Caesar may have modified his operations and tactics after discovering the alleged lack of tenacity of these Belgian warriors in battle. (Austin. *Exploratio...,* p.14).

[101] 'In an intelligence context, markets and trading-stations are also listening posts' (Austin. *Exploratio...,* p.27). 'In a world which lacked more sophisticated modes of communication, therefore, the market-place played an important role in the dissemination of news' (Lee. *Op. Cit.,* p.176).

[102] Austin. *Exploratio...,* p.32.

[103] Piekalkiewicz explains this corroboration by stating that 'among the inhabitants, shepherds and hunters were generally considered to have the best knowledge of the terrain. If one doubted their reliability and loyalty they were closely observed and, if necessary, taken along in bonds. In addition to guides, where possible, deserters and prisoners were used to verify and interpret the information obtained' (Piekalkiewicz. *Op. Cit.*, p.109).

[104] See Ammianus,XV,10,11; XVI,12,2; XVII,1,8; XIX,5,5; XX,4,1; XXI,7,7; XXI,13,4; XXV,7,1 and XXIX,4,2 which are some of the examples referred to later in this book.

[105] Ammianus,XIV,10,7.

[106] Ammianus,XVI,11,9.

[107] Ammianus,XVII,1,8 and AUSTIN. *Ammianus...*, p.69 to 80.

[108] Ammianus specifies that the autumnal equinox, i.e., 22 or 23 September, has passed and that there is snow on the ground (Ammianus,XVII,1,10).

[109] At the Battle of Strasbourg, Ammianus states that Julian mobilized only about 13,000 soldiers to face the 35,000–strong Alamanni attackers (Ammianus,XVI,12,2 to 26). Ferrill supports this number of Roman troops (Ferrill. *The Fall...*, p.66).

[110] Ammianus, XVI,12,64.

[111] Ammianus, XIX,5,5.

[112] Ammianus, XVIII,5,3. 'Voulant échapper aux poursuites de créanciers puissants et impitoyables, il traversa le Tigre avec sa famille, et se mit à la disposition du roi de perse. Avant de partir, il s'était renseigné exactement sur l'état de l'armée romaine et sur la force des places' (Dautremer. *Op. Cit.*, p.20).

[113] We offer the interested reader a classic example of document capture resulting in a great strategic and operational advantage for the Romans with the Battle of Metaurus in 207 BCE. The Roman general Claudius Nero knew the Carthaginians's dispositions after having captured the bearer of a letter from Hasdrubal addressed to Hannibal. The Roman general then defeated Hasdrubal before the two Carthaginian forces were able to be grouped. For more details, see the book Baldelli G. Paci E. Tomassini L. *La Battaglia del Metauro, Testi, Tesi, Ipotesi*, Fano, Italia, Minardi Editore, 1994, 186p. It is obviously implied that the

beneficiary of such documents must also assess the possibility of a disinformation manoeuvre on the part of his opponent.

[114] Austin. *Exploratio...,* p.111.

[115] 'To this day, any cipher alphabet that consists of the standard sequence, like Caesar's, is called a Caesar alphabet' (Kahn D. (1996) *The Code Breakers*, New York, Scribner, p.83–84). Trombley suggests that Procopius used another type of code, the cipher, which refers in this context to the use of any sort of obscure allusions relating to classical historical literature that only a well-educated person could resolve (Drijvers. *Op. Cit.*, p.22.).

[116] Augustus 'made a revolutionary step in the history of Roman intelligence by founding a regular service assured by special messengers (...) which existed up to the end of the Roman Empire' (Dvornik. *Op. Cit.*, p.91 et 92).

[117] 'These wayside inns were run primarily for the imperial post and in many cases included a bathhouse for the weary, dusty traveller' (Mengel M. et Murpphy D. (April 2001) 'A Rural Lycian Bath House, Abstract', *American Journal of Archaeology*, 105,2, p.262).

[118] Dvornik. *Op. Cit.*, p.100. These distances are also reported by Piekalkiewicz (Piekalkiewicz. *Op. Cit.,* p.107).

[119] Dvornik specifies that the *frumentarii* 'became also the most convenient instrument for policing the population. and controlling and influencing public opinion'. It was also the responsibility of the *frumentarii* to ensure the proper functioning of the *Cursus publicus* (Dvornik. *Op. Cit.,* p.101 et 107). Ferrill adds that 'if one were to compare them to a modern American institution, it would be to say that they had some of the characteristics of military intelligence

and of the Federal Bureau of Investigation (FBI)' (Neilson. *Op. Cit.,* p.18).

[120] Besnier M. (1937) *L'Empire romain de l'avènement des Sévères au Concile de Nicée*, Paris, Presses Universitaires de France, p.197. It seems reasonable to assume that the *frumentarii* were present in all provinces of the Empire. It is also plausible to believe that there was a concentration of agents in the cities hosting the imperial residences such as Rome and Constantinople (Istanbul). Rolfe explains in the lexicon of volume one that the *frumentarii* posted to Rome were housed in the *Castra peregrina*, in the heart of the city. Bunson supports this statement and adds that a temple to Jupiter was kept in the camp, and that it stood there as late as 357 CE. (Bunson. *Encyclopedia...*, p.77).

[121] 'By the third century under increased pressure to guarantee the flow of revenue in kind and to protect the security of an increasing impoverished and disintegrating state (it should be remembered that the Empire had just gone through the dark period of military anarchy which lasted from 235 to 284), the *frumentarii* became hateful to Rome's subjects. The temptations to exceed their authority also became greater' (Sheldon. *Tinker, Tailor...*, p.174). Ind and Dvornik go as far as comparing them to Hitler's Gestapo (Ind A. (1963) *A Short History of Espionage*, New York, David McKay, p.21; Dvornik. *Op. Cit.,* p.108). Bunson. *Encyclopedia...*, p.164.

[122] Diocletian is probably responsible for the establishment of the *agentes*, although the latter are only mentioned for the first time under the reign of Constantine I in one of his decrees of 319 (Dvornik. *Op. Cit.*, p.129). '*Les chargés de mission :* haïs de la population, les frumentaires, centurions

détachés auprès des préfets du prétoire pour accomplir des besognes de police, avaient été supprimés par Dioclétien (Aurélius Victor, 39, 44). Il les remplaça peut-être par un nouveau corps de chargés de mission, les *agentes in rebus*. Toutefois, cette création pourrait seulement dater du règne de Constantin, époque où est attesté le premier titulaire.' (Rémy. *Op. Cit.*, p.51.

[123] It was 'another service organization for the same counterintelligence/security task' (Sheldon. *Tinker, Tailor...*, p.175). The *agents* also inherited from the *frumentarii* the responsibility for the *cursus publicus* adds Bunson (Bunson. *Encyclopedia...*, p.255). This aspect of continuity with the *frumentarii* is also supported by Ammianus (Ammianus,XIV,11,19).

[124] Delmaire. *Op. Cit.,* p.101.

[125] Delmaire. *Op. Cit.,* p.100.

[126] Delmaire. *Op. Cit.*, p.99. Dvornik. *Op. Cit.,* p.109. Rolfe adds that the *agentes* 'were organized and dressed as soldiers and divided into five grades, with regular promotion from the lowest to the highest; and they sometimes rose to still higher positions. They were at first under the pretorian prefect; after Constantine, under the master of the Offices' (Ammianus. tome 1, p.576). The *magister officiorum* was a very influential figure with the emperor.

[127] Delmaire. Op. Cit., p.30–31. In his introduction, Rolfe states about the members of the *consilium principis* that 'the emperors gathered about them a body of advisers which entirely superseded the senate in importance. It was first called the auditorium or *consilium principis*, but Constantine gave it the title of *consistorium principisor*

sacrum' (Ammianus. tome 1, p.XXIX). In the fourth century, senatorial authority, definitively removed from the high sphere of imperial power, was restricted to the municipal or local level. Bunson defines the *consilium principis* as the 'Council of the State, the body of advisors who helped the emperors decide important legal and administrative matters' (Bunson. *Encyclopedia...*, p. 106). In the fourth century, the *consistorium principisor* was made of high imperial dignitaries, which included the *magister officiorum*.

[128] Sinnigen W. (1961) 'Two Branches of the Late Roman Secret Service', *American Journal of Philology*, 80, p.240 and Dvornik. *Op. Cit.,* p.130.

[129] Ferrill A. (1991) *Roman Imperial Grand Strategy*, Lanham, University Press of America, p.56. The Theodosian Code reveals that there were 1174 *agentes* working within the Empire in 438 (Theodosian Code 6,27,23) and according to the Justinian Code, during the reign of Leo I (457–474), there were 1248 (Justinian Code 12,20,3). Delmaire. *Op. Cit.*, p.101.

[130] Delmaire. *Op. Cit.*, p.102.

[131] Delmaire. *Op. Cit.*, p.103–106.

[132] Delmaire. *Op. Cit.*, p.103–104. They also served as imperial observers at synods and councils in the fifth century.

[133] Dvornik. *Op. Cit.,* p.130.

[134] Ammianus,XVI,5,11.

[135] 'The reputation for slander and intrigue attributed to the corps of the *agentes* was so great that the Emperor Julian discharged almost the entire schola' (Sinnigen. *Two...*, p.245). Dvornik adds that 'Julian, moved by the complaints

voiced by the people of the provinces who had been grossly exploited by the *agentes*, limited their numbers to seventeen. This restriction lasted only during his reign' (Dvornik. *Op. Cit.,* p.130). Delmaire. *Op. Cit.*, p.101.

[136] Ammianus,XXII,3,6 and Ammianus,XXII,7,5.

[137] In the *Res Gestae*, Rolfe translates *notarius* using the terms 'secretary' and 'stenographer'.

[138] 'The internal organization of the corps, like that of the *agentes in rebus*, was the responsibility of the Master of the Offices (*Magister officiorum*)' (Sinnigen. *Two*..., p.241). See also Bunson. *Encyclopedia*..., p.255 and 378; and Delmaire. *Op. Cit.,* p.56.

[139] 'Dès le Haut-Empire, les conseillers étaient assistés de secrétaires de séances esclaves ou affranchis, les notaires, qui rédigeaient les comptes rendus des séances. Hommes de confiance, ils étaient instruits de tous les secrets de d'États. Pendant la tétrarchie, ils furent des hommes libres, rattachés aux bureaux palatins.' (Rémy B. (1998) *Dioclétien et la tétrarchie, « Que sais-je? »*, Presses Universitaires de France, p.47). 'L'administration proprement dite fut partagée entre une *schola* des notaires (ceux qui prennent des notes) sous le *primicier*, et des *scrinia* (bureaux) sous des *magistri*, eux-mêmes soumis à un questeur.' (Le Bohec. *Op. Cit.*, p.110).

[140] Delmaire. *Op. Cit.,* p.49.

[141] Delmaire. *Op. Cit.*, p.44–53.

[142] Neilson. *Op. Cit.,* p.19. Eventually, as states Sinnigen, 'although the original purposes for which the two corps were founded differed, their activities inevitably tended to converge (…) each corps had a reputation for ferreting out information of interest to the government' (Sinnigen.

Two..., p.242 to 245).

[143] Sheldon. *Tinker, Tailor...*, p.182.

[144] Delmaire. *Op. Cit.,* p.51.

[145] Barnes T.D. (1998) *Ammianus Marcellinus and the Representation of Historical Reality*, Ithaca, New York, Cornell University Press, p. 60–63; Ammianus Marcellinus (1935) *Res Gestae*, translation J.C. Rolfe, tome I, Cambridge, Loeb Classical Library, p.IX; Blockley R.C. (1975) *Ammianus Marcellinus: A Study of his Historiography and Political Thought*, coll. Latomus, vol. 141, Bruxelles, Revues d'études latines, p.8; Dautremer L. (1899) *Ammien Marcellin*, « Études d'histoire littéraire », tome VII, Lille, Presses universitaires de Lille, p.7.

[146] Crump. *Op. Cit.*, p.1.

[147] When Augustus became the first emperor of the Romans in 27 BC, he set up a personal guard which he named the Praetorian Guard. Throughout the period of the Principate, the size of the guard varied between 5,000 and 10,000 elite soldiers. The commander of this guard, the praetorian prefect, was one of the most influential individuals after the emperor. Around 320 CE, Constantine I dissolved the Praetorian Guard and replaced it with the *protectores domesticus*, formed by troops whose loyalty was more reliable. The latter were under the authority of the *comes domesticorum*. The position of the praetorian prefect was maintained, but his role was redefined and restricted mainly to tasks related to the high imperial administration. Until the time of Constantine I, a military palatine official, the praetorian prefect became an exclusively civilian provincial official. (Delmaire. *Op. Cit.*, p.173). Ammianus probably enrolled into the *protectores domesticus* around 350.

(Ammianus. tome 1, p.XLIII; Bunson M. (1991) *A Dictionary of the Roman Empire*, New York, Oxford University Press, p.354; Barnes. *Op. Cit.*, p.1).

[148] Austin. N. (1979) *Ammianus on Warfare: An Investigation into Ammianus' Military Knowledge*, coll. Latomus, vol. 165, Bruxelles, Revue d'études latines, p.13.

[149] Crump. *Op. Cit.*, p.12; Drijvers. *Op. Cit.*, p.17–18, 59; Austin. *Ammianus...*, p.7 and 22.

[150] Dautremer. *Op. Cit.*, p.13; Bunson M. (1994) *Encyclopedia of the Roman Empire*, New York, Facts On File, p.135.

[151] Ursicinus also fought in Gaul during this period. (Southern P. and Dixon K. (1996) *The late Roman Army*, New Haven, Yale University Press, p.39).

[152] Drijvers. *Op. Cit.*, p.21.

[153] Austin specifies about Ammianus that 'many of his modern critics have not hesitated to see fourth-century history through his eyes' (Austin. *Ammianus...*, p.7). Southern adds that the *Res Gestae* represents 'one of the main sources, if not THE main source' (Southern. *Op. Cit.*, p.39).

[154] Crump. *Op. Cit.*, p.131.

[155] *Ibid.*, p.34.

[156] Ammianus. tome I, p.XIV.

[157] Ammianus. tome 3, p.V. Tacitus lived from year 55 to 120, while Dante was born in 1265 and passed away in 1321.

[158] Crump. *Op. Cit.*, p.1.

[159] Ammianus,XIV,6,4.

[160] Gibbon E. (1993) *The Decline and Fall of the Roman Empire*, tome 3, Toronto, Alfred A. Knopf, edition, p.65.

[161] In Ammianus,XVII,7,1 to 14, Ammianus explains the perception of the Roman intelligentsia at the time. This reflects the thinking of Aristotle as set out in his treatise *Meteorologica*. According to Aristotle, an earthquake is caused by the effect of water and wind rushing into caves and caverns on the surface.

[162] Ammianus's explanation of a rainbow is an example: 'The warmer exhalations of the earth and its moist vapours are condensed into clouds; these are then dissipated into a fine spray, which, made brilliant by the sun's rays that fall upon it' (Ammianus,XX,11,26). This definition seems more credible than the one proposing the rainbow as a glowing reflection emanating from a gold coin-filled cauldron hidden at the bottom of a cave surrounded by bouncing overexcited leprechauns…

[163] 'And if it is not known with what male any female tree is in love, her trunk is smeared with her own perfume, and the other tree by a law of nature is attracted by the sweet odour. It is from these signs that the belief in a kind of copulation is created' (Ammianus,XXIV,3,12 et 13).

[164] See Ammianus,XXIII,6,85 to 87 and Ammianus,XX,3,1 to 12.

[165] 'In fact, a whole band of foreigners will be unable to cope with one of them (speaking about a Gaul) in a fight, if he calls in his wife, stronger than he by far and with flashing eyes; least of all when she swells her neck and gnashes her teeth, and poising her huge white arms, proceeds to rain punches mingled with kicks, like shots discharged by the twisted cords of a catapult' (Ammianus,XV,12,1).

[166] Barnes. *Op. Cit.*, p.166.

[167] *Ibid.*, p.198, 232.

[168] Drijvers. *Op. Cit.*, p.110.

[169] Piekalkiewicz. *Op. Cit.*, p.105 and 110.

[170] 'The emperor finally decided, after favouring first one plan then another, to bring about their destruction through the Burgundians, a warlike people, rich in the strength of countless young warriors' (Ammianus,XXVIII,5,9).

[171] As Sheldon states: 'modern historians have been slow to recognize the extent to which the Romans practised covert intelligence techniques. Terms familiar to modern intelligence personnel such as political influence operations, seeding, propaganda, political patronage, safe havens, political assassinations, and paramilitary operations all had their counterparts in ancient Rome' (Sheldon. *The Ancient Imperative....*, p.299).

[172] 'Among many other cares, his first and principal aim was to capture alive by violence or by craft king Macrianus (…) having learned from the reports of deserters where the said king, who expected no hostile move, could be seized' (Ammianus,XXIX,4,2). A dozen years earlier, with the help of a *notarius* named Philagrius, Julian had achieved this kind of feat. (Ammianus,XXI,4,1 to 6). We will return to this in the next chapter on the master spies of the fourth century.

[173] 'For since king Vithicabius (…) again and again kindled the flames of war against us, no efforts were spared to dispose of him by any possible manner of death. And because after attempts he could in no way be overcome or treacherously surrendered, he was slain by the perfidy of an attendant on his private life through the earnest solicitation of our men' (Ammianus,XXVII,10,3–4).

[174] Ammianus,XXX,1,18.

[175] Ammianus,XXX,1,20.

[176] Sheldon. *The Ancient Imperative...*, p.311.

[177] In that sense, Dvornik states that 'the documentary evidence is very scarce' (Dvornik. *Op. Cit.,* p.110). Sheldon goes as far as stating that 'the *frumentarii* and *agentes in rebus* were bureaucrats used as spies and for internal spying only. There is no clear example of them being used as infiltrators (...) The Roman intelligence network served almost exclusively for internal security' (Sheldon. *Tinker, Tailor...*, p.183–184).

[178] Neilson. *Op. Cit.*, p.21. Lee, who is referring to the sixth century historian Procopius of Caesarea (not to be confused with the *notarius* Procopius referred to in this book) who stated that 'it has long been the practice of both Romans and the Persians to support spies at public expense. These men are accustomed to go secretly among the enemy to examine their affairs accurately reporting to their rulers on their return' (Lee. *Op. Cit.,* p.170–171).

[179] Neilson. *Op. Cit.*, p.20. This point is also supported by Sinnigen. *Two...*, p.248.

[180] 'We know that the army intelligence service, at least from Caesar's time, was performed by the *speculatores*, or scouts' (Dvornik. Op. Cit., p.101). Piekalkiewicz adds that 'in each of Caesar's legions were ten specially chosen, well trained spies or scouts. Their task was to accompany the cavalry far in front, or on the enemy flanks, to obtain information about the enemy's country and the population living in the area of operations' (Piekalkiewicz. *Op. Cit.*, p.103).

[181] 'In military operations, reconnaissance or scouting is the exploration of an area by military forces to obtain

information about enemy forces, terrain, and other activities (…) Espionage is usually considered to be different from reconnaissance, as it is performed by non-uniformed personnel operating behind enemy lines'

(https://en.wikipedia.org/wiki/Reconnaissance); 'military observation of a region to locate an enemy or ascertain strategic features' (Oxford Languages); 'a search made for useful military information in the field, especially by examining the ground'

(https://www.dictionary.com/browse/reconnaissance); 'is the activity of obtaining military information about a place by sending soldiers or planes there, or by the use of satellites'

(https://www.collinsdictionary.com/dictionary/english/rec onnaissance); 'a preliminary survey to gain information' (https://www.merriam-webster.com/dictionary/ reconnaissance).

[182] Rolfe translated both Latin terms of *speculatore* and *exploratore* by using the term *scout*. Here are some examples: *verus indicat explorator* = trustworthy scout (Ammianus,XXIX,5,40); *speculatores vero* = scouts (XXI,13,4); *exploratores* = scouts (XXI,7,7); *specutionibus fidis* = trusty scouts (XIV,2,15); *speculatione didicit fida* = trustworthy scouting party (XXVII,2,2); *exploratorum* = scouts (XXV,7,1). Consultations in a Latin/French dictionary also confound these terms by defining both terms as *éclaireur* (scout) and *espion* (spy) (Gariel A. (1939) *Dictionnaire Latin-Français*, collection Portefeuille, Librairie Hatier, Paris, p.224 and 631).

[183] As an example, when describing the role of the *exploratores*, Bunson underlines the dual role of the latter

by stating that they were 'very useful on campaigns to patrol the regions around an advancing legion. On the frontier they were also used in maintaining watch on troublesome tribes or on other kingdoms' (Bunson. *Encyclopedia....*, p.152.). On the other hand, Austin insists on the responsibilities of the *exploratores* as being linked to military reconnaissance by stating that they were 'more clearly involved in gaining advance intelligence than in providing a forward force of skirmishers' (Austin. *Ammianus...*, p.42.).

[184] As Bunson states, 'the *speculatores* never evolved into an empire-wide intelligence organization, such as the *frumentarii*' (Bunson. *Encyclopedia...*, p.394).

[185] Lee. *Op. Cit.,* p.170 and 171; Delmaire. *Op. Cit.,* p.99.

[186] Dvornik. *Op. Cit.,* p.117.

[187] Ammianus,XVII,1,4.

[188] Ammianus,XVIII,2,2 to 7.

[189] In terms of the line of though aiming to minimize the importance of the *Arcanii* in espionage activities, Dvornik underlines the fact that 'there is only one single piece of evidence from the fourth century, reserved by Ammianus Marcellinus from which we may conclude that agents existed' (Dvornik. *Op. Cit.*, p.117).

[190] Ammianus,XXVIII,3,8.

[191] *The Arcanii do seem to have provided some foreign intelligence* (Ferrill. *Roman...*, p.57).

[192] These areas correspond to the region generally located northwest of the Indus River.

[193] Ammianus,XVIII,4,1 and 2.

[194] 'He proceeded to Edessa, a city strongly fortified and well supplied with provisions; there he waited for a time, until scouts or deserters should give information of the

moving of the enemy' (Ammianus,XXI,7,7).

[195] Drijvers. *Op. Cit.*, p. 24. 'To him I was sent with a centurion of tried loyalty, for the purpose of getting better informed of what was going on; and I reached him over pathless mountains and through steep defiles'. Ammianus,XVIII,6,21.

[196] 'But the scouts and deserters who appeared from time to time brought conflicting accounts, being uncertain what would happen, because among the Persians plans are communicated to none save the grandees, who are reticent and loyal' (Ammianus,XXI,13,4).

[197] Ammianus,XVIII,6,16.

[198] 'Constantius was hastening to lend aid to the Orient, which was likely soon to be disturbed by the inroads of the Persians as deserters reported in agreement with our scouts' (Ammianus,XX,4,1).

[199] Ammianus,XX,9,9.

[200] It is likely that the Persians were aware that a Roman counter-offensive was imminent. However, according to Ammianus, they did not know when it would start, and which invasion route the Roman army would take. 'Then, uniting his forces, he marched to Mesopotamia so rapidly that, since no report of his coming had preceded him—for he (Julian) had carefully guarded against that—he came upon the Assyrians unaware' (Ammianus,XXIII,2,7).

[201] 'The emperor was on the point of leaving the spot, when a trustworthy informant reported that in some dark and hidden pits near the walls of the destroyed city, such as are numerous in these parts, a band of the enemy was treacherously lying in wait, intending to rush out unexpectedly and attack the rear of our army'

(Ammianus,XXIV,4,29).

[202] This term, frequently used by modern military strategists and tacticians, suggests a relatively orderly retreat rather than a stampede or rout.

[203] Ammianus states that Sapor II 'learned from the true accounts of scouts and deserters of the brave deeds of our men and the shameful defeats of his army (…) this news filled his mind with fear (…) aware that his own subjects, after the loss of so many men were in a state of extreme panic' (Ammianus,XXV,7,2). It is difficult to verify whether this statement is based on reliable information obtained by the Romans, which still seems plausible, or whether it is a more personal interpretation of events on the part of Ammianus. On the precarious situation of the Roman army Drijvers states that 'at the moment Jovian came to the throne, the Roman army was far from safety, faced intense Persian pressure and was beginning to starve' (Drijvers. *Op. Cit.*, p.109).

[204] 'To gain a free passage, the ruler (Jovian) therefore agreed to surrender five provinces in upper Mesopotamia' (Crump. *Op. Cit.*, p.58).

[205] Syme adds that 'Sapor was not for long appeased by the territories he extorted from Julian's successor. Quarrels arose about Armenia, and Valens undertook an expedition. Yet an accommodation emerged at last. Theodosius in 387, in constraint on other fronts, made a firm pact with the Persians' (Syme R. (1968) *Ammianus and the Historia Augusta*, Oxford, Clarendon Press, p.39).

[206] General Theodosius was the father of the future emperor of the same name who ruled the East and then both parts of the Empire from 378 to 395. The importance of North

Africa lies in the fact that thanks to its rich grain belt, it supplied the western part of the Roman Empire with grain (Crump. *Op. Cit.*, p.54).

[207] Ammianus,XXIX,5,4.

[208] As Gibbon puts it: 'Africa had been lost by the vices of Romanus; it was restored by the virtues of Theodosius'. (Gibbon. *The Decline...*, tome 2, p.573).

[209] 'The attention of the emperor was most seriously engaged by the important intelligence which he received from the civil and military officers who were intrusted with the defence of the Danube' (Gibbon. *The Decline...*, tome 3, p.33).

[210] Ammianus,XXXI,11,2.

[211] '...that his Imperial colleague be awaited, so that, strengthened by the addition of the Gallic army, he might the more easily crush the fiery over-confidence of the barbarians' (Ammianus,XXXI,12,6.).

[212] Ammianus,XXXI,12,11.

[213] Ammianus,XXXI,12,2.

[214] Crump. *Op. Cit.*, p.92. Goldsworthy specifies that the army of Valens was composed of about 20,000 men. (Goldsworthy. *Op. Cit.*, p.183).

[215] 'Valens was in fact given the correct figure for the Gothic forces and that the decision to attack was taken quickly in the light of the fact that only the Gothic infantry under Fritigern was in the vicinity'. (Austin. *Ammianus...*, p.77).

[216] Piekalkiewicz. *Op. Cit.*, p.105 and 110.

[217] Blockley. *Op. Cit.*, p.54.

[218] Ammianus,XXXI,12,1. Gibbon also supports this and blames the defeat to the rash and jealous vanity of Valens.

(Gibbon. *The Decline...*, tome 3, p.60). Barnes also agrees by stating that 'Valens made the catastrophic decision to fight rather than to wait for the arrival of the western emperor Gratian, who was hastening to reinforce him, because of his own obstinacy and the flattery of his courtiers, who urged him not to share with his nephew a victory already as good as won, (Barnes. *Op. Cit.*, p.183). The young Augustus Gratian had indeed inflicted a serious defeat on the Alamanni the previous year (Ammianus,XXXI,10,1 to 22). 'The defeat was largely the result of Valens's mistakes and not of the army's inefficiency' concludes Goldsworthy (Goldsworthy. *Op. Cit.*, p.192).

[219] Austin. *Exploratio...,* p.243. 'For the most part, Romans in the days of the Empire had a perfectly good Secret Service and an adequate system of military intelligence' (Neilson. *Op. Cit.,* p.26).

[220] Ammianus writes about the vulnerability of Constantius II and the cruelty of Paulus, stating: 'and this fatal fault of cruelty, which in others sometimes grew less with advancing age, in his (Constantius II) case became more violent, since a group of flatterers intensified his stubborn resolution. Prominent among these was the state secretary Paulus, a native of Spain, a kind of viper, whose countenance concealed his character, but who was extremely clever in scenting out hidden means of danger for others' (Ammianus,XIV,5,5 et 6). In the *Res Gestae*, Ammianus's perception of Constantius II is rather unfavourable. As Whitby argues, 'although he (Constantius II) is accorded a fair amount of praise, the overall impression is unfavourable' (Drijvers. *Op. Cit.*, p.77).

[221] Delmaire. *Op. Cit.*, p. 53.

[222] Ammianus,XIX,12,1.

[223] Ammianus,XIV,5,6. Dautremer eloquently explains that Paulus was referred to in this way '*pour l'habileté qu'il mettait à serrer fortement les nœuds de la calomnie*' (Dautremer. *Op. Cit.*, p.131).

[224] For a concise but complete description of Magnentius's reign, see Bartolini M. *Roman Emperors...*, p.108–110.

[225] Ammianus,XIV,5,4 to 8.

[226] Blockley. *Op. Cit.,* p.18.

[227] Ammianus,XV,3,1.

[228] Barnes. *Op. Cit.*, p.131.

[229] Ammianus,XV,6,1; Bunson. *Encyclopedia...*, p.389; Ammianus,XV,5,31; Ammianus,XV,5,4.

[230] Ammianus,XXII,3,10 and 11.

[231] Ammianus,XIV,11,19.

[232] Ammianus,XIV,11,23.

[233] Ammianus,XV,1,2.

[234] Ammianus,XV,5,8.

[235] Barnes. *Op. Cit.*, p.132.

[236] Ammianus,XV,3,8; Delmaire. *Op. Cit.*, p. 110.

[237] As Syme puts it, 'the guests uttered freely their discontent with the present order of things'. (Syme. *Op. Cit.*, p.66).

[238] Ammianus,XV,3,10.

[239] Ammianus,XVII,9,7.

[240] This designation is also supported by Sinnigen (Sinnigen. *Two...*, p.245).

[241] Ammianus,XXI,7,2.

[242] Ammianus,XXII,11,1.

[243] 'By some craft or other to stay Sapor's preparations, so

that his northern provinces might not be fortified beyond the possibility of attack'. (Ammianus,XVII,5,15).

[244] 'And this was the plan that he (Julian) formed. He had sent to those regions his secretary, Philagrius, later Count of the Orient, in whose good judgement he had confidence, having already tested it (…) As soon as the feast was ended, he laid a strong hand on Vadomarius and handed him over to the commander of the soldiers to be closely confined in camp' (Ammianus,XXI,4,1 to 6).

[245] Hostilities resumed the following year when the Alamanni again began to plunder the border areas of the Empire. The Alamanni remained a threat to the Empire until the end of the fourth century.

[246] Gibbon. *The Decline…*, tome 2, p.368. See Bartolini M. *Roman Emperors…*, p.105–108 and Drijvers. *Op. Cit.*, p.23.

[247] Ammianus,XX,4,2.

[248] Ammianus,XX,4,1 to 22.

[249] Ammianus,XXIV,4,21.

[250] Ammianus,XXIV,4,23.

[251] Ammianus,XXVI,6,3; Bunson. *Encyclopedia…*, p.297.

[252] Ammianus,XXV,8,18.

[253] Ammianus,XXVIII,6,12. This is a perfect example of a 'covert operation'.

[254] Ammianus,XXVIII,6,17.

[255] 'Palladius then came to an understanding with Romanus, and on his return to the palace, he misled Valentinian by the atrocious art of lying, declaring that the people of Tripoli had no cause for complaint'. (Ammianus,XXVIII,6,20).

[256] Ammianus,XXVIII,6,22 and 23.

[257] Ammianus,XXVIII,6,25.

[258] Ammianus,XXVIII,6,27.

[259] Ammianus,XXVI,5,14.

[260] 'Not a single man survived to tell what had happened, except Syagrius. He, after all the others had been slain, returned to the court, but by sentence of the angry emperor he was cashiered and went to his home, being considered by a cruel judgement to have deserved this because he alone had escaped'. (Ammianus,XXVIII,2,9).

[261] Ammianus,XXVIII,2,5.

[262] Ammianus,XXIX,1,7.

[263] About this, Blockley states that 'by the fourth century A.D. superstition and belief had to a considerable extent displaced reason' (Blockley. *Op. Cit.,* p.105).

[264] Bartolini M. *Roman Emperors...,* p.117–120.

[265] Blockley. *Op. Cit.,* p.119.

[266] Ammianus,XXIX,2,5.

[267] Delmaire. *Op. Cit.*, p. 54; Ammianus,XXIX,1,6.

[268] Ammianus,XXIX,1,1 to 44.

[269] Syme. *Op. Cit.*, p.32; Dautremer. *Op. Cit.*, p.13.

[270] Ammianus,XXIX,1,11.

[271] Ammianus,XXIX,1,10; Dautremer. *Op. Cit.*, p.81; Gibbon. *The Decline...*, tome 2, p.530.

[272] Ammianus,XXVIII,1,10.

[273] 'And he associated with him in the investigation of these charges which were being devised for the peril of many the secretary Leo' (Ammianus,XXVIII,1,12). Ammianus did not seem to like Leo, whom he described later in the *Res Gestae* as a 'wild beast' (Ammianus,XXX,2,10), but gave no further explanation.

[274] Ammianus,XXX,2,10; Ammianus,XXX,5,10.

[275] Ammianus,XXVIII,1,57.

[276] Ammianus,XXX,3,2.

[277] Bartolini M. *Roman Emperors...*, p.114–117.

[278] Ammianus,XXVI,6,1.

[279] Procopius would have been a cousin of Julian. (Ammianus,XXVI,6,1; Sinnigen. *Two...*, p.244; Bunson. *Encyclopedia...*, p.349; et Blockley. *Op. Cit.,* p.55).

[280] 'Strict on his life and character, although retiring and silent, he served for a long time with distinction as state-secretary' (Ammianus,XXVI,6,1).

[281] 'Afterward Count Lucillianus was dispatched, together with Procopius, at that time state secretary, to accomplish the self-same thing (the *status quo*) with like insistence on the conditions' (Ammianus,XVII,14,3).

[282] As we have already mentioned, it was undoubtedly to assess the state of the Persian war preparations.

[283] Ammianus,XVIII,6,17.

[284] Ammianus,XXVI,6,1. Bunson explains that the counts are 'the leading officials of the Roman Empire. They wielded posts of every description, from the army to the civil service, while never surrendering their direct links and access to the emperors' (Bunson. *Encyclopedia....*, p.102).

[285] Ammianus,XXIII,3,5. Gibbon specifies that 'Procopius had been hastily promoted from the obscure station of a tribune and a notary to the joint command of the army of Mesopotamia' (Gibbon. *The Decline...*, tome 2, p.529).

[286] 'Julian instantly put 30,000 picked men under the command of the aforesaid Procopius, and joined to him with equal powers Sebastianus' specifies Ammianus (Ammianus,XXIII,3,5). Sinnigen supports these numbers of 30,000 (Sinnigen. Two..., p.247); on the other hand, Austin proposes that the army of Procopius had rather 20,000 soldiers and that the one led by Julian in Persian

territory had 40,000 (Austin. Ammianus…, p.95) for a total of 60,000 soldiers. As for Gibbon, the latter suggests an army totalling 65,000 soldiers (Gibbon. *The Decline*…, tome 2, p.473).

[287] Ferrill. *The Fall*…, p.53.

[288] Austin. *Ammianus*…, p.96.

[289] Ammianus,XXV,7,13. Details on the ratification of this treaty have already been discussed in Chapter 3.

[290] 'With no witness present, Julian is said secretly to have handed his purple mantle to his relative Procopius, and to have ordered him boldly to assume the rule, if he learned that the emperor had died among the Parthians'. (Ammianus,XXIII,3,2). Gibbon summarizes the controversy surrounding Procopius simply by saying that 'a vain rumour was propagated by his friends or his enemies' (Gibbon. *The Decline*…, tome 2, p.529).

[291] Gibbon. *The Decline*…, tome 2, p.514. This was done according to Julian's wishes. Ammianus explains Jovian's suspicious attitude by writing: 'a band of flatterers pressed upon the timid emperor, harping upon the dreaded name of Procopius, and declaring that if he returned (…) he would with the fresh troops under his command easily and without opposition make himself emperor' (Ammianus,XXV,7,10).

[292] Ammianus,XXVI,6,3. As Ammianus states: 'he disappeared and in spite of the most careful search could not be found anywhere' (Ammianus,XXV,9,12 and 13).

[293] Ammianus,XXVI,6,6.

[294] Bartolini M. *Roman Emperors*…, p.113–114.

[295] Blockley. *Op. Cit.,* p.56.

[296] All this Procopius observed from his hiding-place, and thinking that when a more favourable turn of fortune should

occur, the crown of supreme power could be gained with little trouble (Ammianus,XXVI,6,10).

[297] Ammianus,XXVI,6,12 to 14.

[298] Blockley. *Op. Cit.,* p.55.

[299] Ammianus,XXVI,5,13.

[300] 'He could now boldly invade the oriental provinces without opposition'. (Ammianus,XXVI,8,14).

[301] As Crump states: 'ultimately, the failure of Procopius to enlist an adequate number of dependable soldiers brought victory to Valens' armies' (Crump. *Op. Cit.*, p.55).

[302] 'He was taken to the camp and handed over to the emperor, silent and terror-stricken. He was at once beheaded, and so put an end to the rising storm of civil strife and war'. (Ammianus,XXVI,9,9).

[303] Bartolini M. (2007) 'L'espion devenu empereur : Procope d'après Ammien Marcellin', *Histoire Antique*, Éditions Faton, France, No 31, p.67.

[304] Ammianus,XXVII,2,10.

[305] Delmaire, *Op. Cit.,* p.54.

[306] Dvornik. *Op. Cit.,* p.53.

[307] As Austin states: 'from then on, to at least the end of the fourth century, intelligence was collected much more actively and aggressively' (Austin. *Exploratio…*, p.13).

[308] 'L'empereur disposait d'un conseil (*consilium principis*), réuni d'abord en fonction des nécessités, puis avec régularité à partir d'Hadrien : il était présidé par le préfet du prétoire, il avait une composition fixe et il était formé surtout de juristes et de militaires, parce qu'il intervenait essentiellement dans des affaires requérant ces deux domaines de compétence. Le prince se faisait aider par des institutions qu'on appelle la 'chancellerie', un ensemble

de bureaux ou *officia* (…). Le bureau des comptes (*a rationibus*) était le plus important : il était aidé par les services des archives (*a memoria*), des enquêtes (*a studii*), des requêtes (*a cognitionibus*) et de la correspondance latine et grecque (*ad epistulis latinis et graecis*)'. (Le Bohec. *Op. Cit.*, p.59).

[309] Austin. *Exploratio…*, p.111.

[310] *Ibid.*, p.137. See also Bunson. *Encyclopedia…*, p.147.

[311] Sheldon. (Spring 1993) *Tinker, Tailor…*, p.ix; Sheldon R. 'The Spartacus Rebellion: A Roman Intelligence Failure?', *International Journal of Intelligence and Counterintelligence*, 6, no 1, p.69.

[312] Sinnigen. *Two…*, p.254.

[313] Public Affairs Staff, (February 1994) *A Consumer's guide to Intelligence*, Washington, CIA, PAS94–00039, p.viii. For a more elaborate flowchart of the same process, see Dearth D.H. and Goodden R.T. (1995) *Strategic Intelligence: Theory and Application*, Washington, DIA, PA17013–5050, Second Edition, p.18.

[314] Drijvers. *Op. Cit.*, p.27.

[315] Barnes. *Op. Cit.*, p.60.

[316] Bey F. (Novembre-décembre 2001) 'À la croisée des chemins. L'armée romaine de 117 à 217 ap. J.-C.', Ordre de Bataille, 41, p.27.